The Wind Cried

Oil painting by Umberto Romano

PAUL HECHT

THE DIAL PRESS, INC. New York 1968

An American's Discovery of the World of Flamenco

The Wind Cried

To Elaine:

who stood by me everywhichway

Acknowledgments

Diego Beijveder, Manuel Soto, Ángel Luiggi, and Manuel Ávila: singers who carried me into and through the pages of this book.

La Fernanda de Utrera: who encouraged my love for her art.

Manolito, "él de Maria": who goes his own way.

José Núñez, "Pepe, él de La Matrona": artist and teacher.

Francisco Bejarano Robles: in whose archives there were books and friendship.

José Luque Navajas: who unwaveringly offered me everything he had.

Pepe Navarro: tender incarnation of the superior *aficionado*.

Elías Téres: with a smile on his lips pouring wine.

Antonio Ámado: dreaming of divine sessions in Madrid.

Anselmo González Climent: from San Roque and Buenos Aires, his deep *jaleo* was inspiration and guide.

All my friends in the Peña Juan Breva.

Aubrey David and Ramón Morales: who generously let me live in the farmhouse where I started this book.

My country neighbors: who gave me food and laughter.

Special acknowledgment to José Luque Navajas for basic ideas on the history and evolution of *cante* and to Fernando Montoro for aid in the compilation of the *coplas*.

Contents

The Wind Cried

1

Aquel pajarito, madre
que canta en la verde oliva
dígale usté que se calle
que su cante me lastima.

That little bird, Mother
That sings in the green olive
Tell it to hush
Because its song hurts me.

*D*iego Beijveder Morilla, called "El Pijin" or
"El Perote," was born in 1886 in Álora, a farming town about forty
kilometers northwest of the city of Málaga. Besides having rich
orchards producing lemons, oranges, and muscatel grapes, Álora
nurtured the major creators and interpreters of the *malagueña*; it
was one of those towns, found in every Andalusian province,
where enthusiasm for *cante flamenco* was a heritage sustained by
each generation. At seventeen, Diego came to Málaga, hung around
the *cafés cantantes* where flamenco was the main attraction for the
andaluz of the period, perfected his knowledge of the leading
styles, and began his career as a professional *cantaor*, a singer of

3

cante. He was never a major figure, and after the *cafés cantantes* shut down and flamenco moved into traveling troupes, theatres and night clubs, he hung on in Málaga, eking out an erratic living from private fiestas and the generosity of the *pagano.*[1] He married, had two children, and survived.

I met Diego in the spring of 1960 when the folklorist Sam Eskin asked me to interpret for a recording session. I was living in Fuengirola, a resort town on the Mediterranean, about thirty kilometers southwest of Málaga, and I knew almost nothing about flamenco save that the few times I had heard it I was deeply moved. It was typical of my floating life then that I didn't penetrate the societal surface myself and discover this world, embedded in the Andalusian psyche for at least two hundred years, but that another American, a man whose life is linked to folk music and therefore to people, had to come where I lived and reveal it to me.

We met Diego at the apartment of a friend of Antonio Vargas, the guitarist. I saw a small, nervous, very thin, very old man who looked as if he would crumble if you touched him. I remember he wore a raincoat draped over his shoulders like a cape: his little artistic touch. He put away several glasses of wine right off the bat to ease his nerves. The tape recorder and the microphone were strange metallic bugs, and he leaned in toward the familiarity of his guitar. When he began to sing, Sam and I looked at each other. We knew nothing about flamenco but the *sound* of this old man made the past come alive in the moment of now. There was such a tenderness, "a sad breeze blowing through the olive trees," a particular endurance that was virile and sensitive—it was no sound I'd ever heard before, and looking at Diego with his eyes half closed bringing the music out from the center of his seventy-four years, I responded to him with a smile of joyous admiration.

Now, seven years later, after having heard him many times, alone and with other singers, in varying circumstances, moods, physical conditions, and after having heard a lot of flamenco, I ask myself what it is about his sound that moves me. It's not simply that he's old, because I have heard many old singers who make a small, empty, or false sound. This isn't all of it, but I think that

[1] *Pagano* is flamenco argot meaning "he who pays the artists" and a pun on *pagar* (to pay) and *pagano* (pagan).

the sound is *him at his best*: when his little life of envy, vanity, petulance, and greed has been dissolved; when the snubs, defeats, scorn, and patronizing are submerged, and he makes his sound of a man under an olive tree, a man riding a horse through the sierra, a man picking up a child, a man plowing, a man admiring a beautiful woman, a man *singing*—singing against and beyond the defeats. Because even at the height of his physical powers Diego stayed at the outer rim of the select gatherings: he was a second-rater. And how many nights did he endure when all the *oles* were for others? But when he sings now, his voice almost gone, young and old alike shake their heads in respect and admiration. These thoughts have haunted me throughout my entire involvement with flamenco. If Diego is a second-rater, what kind of sounds did the masters make? And why is Diego's sound different from the younger singers who sing the same songs?

Apart from the personal difference, apart from the fact that the masters and the stylistic influences differ, there is a larger historic difference. When Diego started to sing at the turn of the century he was much closer to the *andaluz* of all previous times, but the young singer of today is cut off from the preceding generations and is a stranger, almost a foreigner, to someone like Diego. The social earth is opening up beneath the young singer. On one side of the abyss is a music that expresses Andalusia from, let's say, 3000 B.C. to 1936 A.D., and on the other side is Andalusia, 1967. His friends are dancing the twist and studying English. He is still *andaluz*: in the innermost streams of his blood he feels a pull; but the sound is strange in 1967 when flamenco singers wear Tyrolean hats and business suits and study chemistry. Think of the early blues singers, Ma Rainey or Bessie Smith, and then think of those young singers singing the blues today. The sound is totally different. I'm not disparaging the young *cantaores*. I'm only pointing up the struggle they have to make to retain the flamenco sound—not merely to imitate the past, but to incorporate their changing values and sensibilities, the new attitudes each generation takes before eternal problems, into the musical forms and sounds of flamenco.

I became aware of this struggle in the national contests. I heard young boys really wailing, executing the styles in a more or less traditional manner, feeling the song, but too often the sound was not flamenco. Diego just tuning up makes it, but the young singers have to hunt for it in a strange, unknown forest. Why? Because the flamenco sound, like the blues sound, is linked to a way of being that has particular historic tensions and durations. In Spanish, not only does someone practice the art of flamenco—he also *is* a flamenco. When Diego begins to sing, *cante* is still in its golden age and the flamenco manner is still an ideal for the *andaluz*, just as the torero, the contrabandist, the highwayman once were. The *cantaor*, in his carriage, social relations, gestures, and thinking lived integrally as a flamenco, that is, as a certain kind of *andaluz*. But in the 1960's, other ideals, other values have penetrated Andalusian society. Flamenco survives, but the young singer has the added dimension of historical consciousness. As he performs more and more in places and for people alien to his way of being, he becomes more and more conscious of himself in the *role* of *cantaor*. Of necessity, he makes extra-flamenco acts. He becomes an entertainer. But the authentic *cantaor* is never an entertainer.

In 1956, in the National Contest of Córdoba, a singer in his early twenties, Antonio Fernández Díaz, "Fosforito," took first prize in all the categories. He was a tremendous revelation, a seemingly anachronistic throwback to an earlier period. He had the classical, hoarse flamenco voice; he knew all the old styles; he sang with depth. "Fosforito" knows more styles than Diego, is more inspired and creative. But Diego, walking through the streets, sitting in his chair smoking, drinking, submerging himself in preparatory rhythms, is more *himself* as a flamenco. In 1961 I saw in "Fosforito's" face and stance a certain uneasiness and self-consciousness; he reminded me of the farmboys I saw trying to have a casual drink in a high-class foreign bar on the Costa del Sol: both "Fosforito" and the boys have been catapulted away from their source, their natural habitat, and placed before faces that understand neither their speech nor their music. But Diego would be flamenco in the White House or on the moon. His being is in perfect balance for the introspection needed to sing flamenco. "Fosforito" is involved in a desperate struggle to reach that equilibrium. To function as a flamenco he needs the intimacy of closed doors and knowing *aficionados*, yet he spends much of his time singing in the theatre and in high society. The problem is one not of change but of abnormal speed of change. In one generation Spain has been hurled into the twentieth century. The new rhythms dance their frenzied dance against millennial ones. The compulsive twitch, the pro- liferation of mask, confront a man rolling a cigarette under an olive tree.

Let's get back to my first meeting with Diego. In the first five or six songs his voice kept getting richer and richer, the variety of feelings wider and deeper; he left his beloved *malagueña* and en- tered the *siguiriya gitana*, a style that is usually the sounding board for the harsh, metallic, unadorned anguish of the gypsies. But with Diego the chant left the tribal campfire, the cave and became a man alone in an olive grove (if I come back again and again to the olive, it's because this tree, as no other, is a root-and-sap reality of An- dalusia) pondering and weeping his fate. Even the *ay*—which in the gypsy is a knife-at-the-throat sound, a chain, a parched throat, a wound—was transformed by Diego into another sound: that of manhood mutilated by time, of a sprig of rosemary, if it could speak, being torn up by the roots, the sound of an old man alone in a café waiting for some life to touch him before death comes. This was the verse:

> *A la medianoche*
> *me despierto y digo:*
> *Pa' qué me sirven tantas cavilaciones*
> *si tú no estás conmigo.*

> At midnight
> I wake up and say:
> What's the use of all this brooding
> If you're not with me.

Then the wine hit him. He drank too fast and too much, his voice broke, he couldn't find the complex tones, and in the rest of the songs his voice was pathetic and maudlin. I couldn't forget the change from a nervous old man (after all, we were strangers, did we know flamenco, did we like it and, more important, would we like *him*) to one who declaimed after hearing his voice on the play- back: "Ole, there's no one from here to Sevilla who can sing these songs." And every ten minutes he kept asking Sam to play them back. I was lucky to be brought into the world of flamenco this way instead of by the usual, hand-clapping, drunken-merry, brawl-ing, festive atmosphere, which has its own merit but which would not have reverberated so deeply within me. At the end of the evening, Diego asked me: "Do you like my singing? Did I sing well?" I was stunned. To be able to sing like that and then to ask me, a stranger, a foreigner, ignorant of his music, if he sang well. It was then I glimpsed the terribly human implications in the world of flamenco. All artists are concerned with the reaction of the "other," but in flamenco, the response *must* be immediate. The listener cannot remain outside the drama. I was to find out that the authentic *cantaor*, professional or *aficionado*, was always trem-bling within with that question: "Do you like my singing? Does it move you?"

Diego toddled off into the night, his arm around the guitarist. Both were high and had money in their pockets. I heard Diego whisper, "Let's find some girls." He was forty years older than I was, and I could hardly stand up from all the wine and the emotion. I thought: Have I stumbled onto a new race of men?

I was bitten; I was sweetly poisoned and I plunged into this new world: I wanted to know and to feel everything about it. So I asked Diego where I could hear authentic flamenco in Málaga, but privately, not in a night club, and he said: "Well, on Saturday nights I get together with some friends in this bar called Casa Luna and we sing there. Come one Saturday and I'll introduce you around." For the next six months, in this bar, with this group of men—actually a formal club called the Peña Juan Breva[2]—I listened to Diego sing, and I began to study the songs and the complex human manifestations of flamenco.

Then, suddenly, Diego was sent to a tuberculosis sanatorium in El Escorial, north of Madrid. The flamencos rumored that he really didn't have T.B. but that his bohemian manner of living was too much for his son, a hard-working bourgeois completely removed from his father's world. "He only likes soccer," Diego once said, as if talking about a cretin. At any rate, with Diego gone the whole temper of the Peña changed. There was no one to sing the old

---

[2] Juan Breva was a great stylist of the *malagueña* in its earlier transitional phase. He died in 1918. Diego never thought of the Peña as a club; for him it was a place "where he and his friends sang."

malagueña. Diego encompasses a period prior to recorded music. Only through men his age do we have some idea of original styles. No matter how good the other singing in the Peña might be, it was always incomplete without his other-century sound.

A year later I went with my sister to visit El Escorial and to see Diego. He didn't recognize me at first. He looked so sad and lonely, but when we spoke about Málaga his whole skinny frame flamed up: "I'm getting out of here, Pablo. One day I'm just going to take off. I'm not spending another winter here; it's a living death. Do you know how cold it gets? *There's snow here.* Well, I'm gonna break away and one Saturday night I'll knock on the door of the Peña and I'll say: 'Can one enter here?' And then I'll sing four or five *malagueñas* and I'll say: 'All right, let's see what these little boys can do after this.' " We walked around the hospital together. They all knew him and his particular Málagan accent and humor. He'd even improvised a *fandango* on one of the nuns:

> *Aquí hay una monjita*
> *salpicada de lunares,*
> *y como la ven tan bonita*
> *todos me la quieren quitar*
> *pero no me la quitan.*

> There's a nun here
> Her face splashed with beauty spots,
> And since she's so pretty
> They all want to take her away from me
> But they can't do it.

We talked about flamenco and he said bitterly, as if in exile on another continent: "Ah, they don't know anything about it here, but when we all take our morning walk outside, I go off on one of the paths and sing to myself." We returned to his room, which he shared with three others. It was empty, and as the cold wind blew in through the open door, he sang with bitterness in his face and voice:

> *Reniego de mi sino*
> *como reniego de mi sino*
> *hasta reniego de la horita*
> *que di contigo.*

I curse my fate
How I curse my luck
I even curse the hour
That I met you.

I had brought him some instant coffee and I gave him some money, telling him it was from the Peña. He looked in my face and asked: "From the Peña or from you?" I answered him with the *copla*:

No preguntes por saber
que el tiempo te lo dirá
no hay cosa más bonita
que el saber sin preguntar.

Don't ask to know
For time will tell it to you
There's nothing nicer
Than knowing without asking.

He laughed and sang it for me knowing that would please me most. I embraced his frail body and said goodbye.

I met my sister for lunch. We were part of a tour that took us from Madrid to see El Escorial and lunch was included. We were fed with the same speed and vulgarity I imagined they would use for the inspection of El Escorial. What a show! Backward Spain was showing the more sophisticated, advanced peoples the highlights of its country. The illusion of travel was in full belt-line motion. Keep 'em moving. If they have time to reflect it might shake the whole foundations of tourism. Travel is to go to see and to be in a country. Tourism is to go and pass by as many objects and landscapes as possible in a given time. The tourist is fed the skin of the grape; the traveler gets the juice inside. A day spent with Diego would reveal more about Spain than ten tours. I sat in the dining room, the din of cowbells clanging in my ears. The cattle were being fed and then would be moved toward the night's camping ground. Diego was eating his lunch alone in the sanatorium.

About six months later I met him in the street in Málaga. He was beaming like a young boy, the wit pouring out of him. We sat down for coffee and he retold tragicomically the story of his "release from jail and how the executioners let him go." He was back in his sunny Málaga, had a new suit, and was a dapper rooster crowing at all hours. He always loved to drink, so when I ordered cognac I was surprised when he said: "No, *chiquillo*, not for me. I don't want them to put me back in jail again."

A week later, in the same café, we were sitting and chatting when he leaned towards me, deadpan: "Pablo, how about a glass of wine to get my throat mellow. You know I can't sing with my blood cold." And he proceeded to get mellow. That night was one of his big nights. At the Peña they played a tape of songs he had recorded two years earlier on a night he had sung well. He was the center of attention, all the *oles* were for him, and for the moment the years of being a second-rater, a hanger-on, of sitting alone in a café waiting for someone to ask him to sing were washed away. We left together, and as I started to say goodbye—it was late and I was tired—he said: "Where you going? It's early. Come on, let's go for a last drink." I asked him about a particular song, whose it was, and he said: "What do you mean, whose song? Don't I have any songs of my own? It's mine." He was high and didn't want it to end, not this night of success; he didn't want to go back to his lonely boardinghouse room, so he took me to a strange bar, but it was after hours, they weren't friendly, and it dampened his good spirits. He gave up and let me go. But he was the same old Diego with an endurance I have no name for. His voice, weak in volume when I first met him, had diminished even more during the time in the sanatorium, but the sound was the same. The olive trees were still there.

Diego is at his best with only two or three witnesses in a quiet place. He knows his voice is almost gone and shies away from noisy gatherings. Being an authentic *cantaor* he thrives in intimate sessions. No matter how subtly I try to draw him out, he rarely talks about the past. He doesn't think in anecdotes. Only when faced with a direct question about his life will he stir himself to answer, and even then I often see on his face: "Doesn't he ever get tired of asking questions?" But what he loves is when I ask him to repeat a verse and I take out my notebook and write it down. Then I am the journalist and he is the celebrity, he the master and I the disciple. He laughs and says: "Why are you always writing down the poems? You think you'll write down all the verses I know?"

He is at his best when he respects his listeners for their knowledge and sensitivity towards his music, and then his half-voice singing vibrates with more emotive force than most excellent shouters. He has had a lifetime of living with his songs, of singing them so many times under varying moods, of having grown up with the great creators and interpreters when every day moved toward the intense drama of nighttime, and now this creative life has finally taken a permanent form and it is his sound.

He sits alone in his café all day, goes alone to the *pensión* at mealtime, and returns there to sleep, alone, at night. Sometimes I or the flamencos of Málaga sit with him or take him off to some quiet place to listen to him sing. Or he sings in the Peña Juan Breva. He lives now as he has always lived: for the moment he is singing. Then the somber, chiseled, Roman face takes on a red flesh color; he blushes like a boy; he laughs, and his wit ranges from the obscene to the tender; he adds a few years to his age and declaims authoritatively about his music. Diego is essentially a *malagueñero*, a singer of *malagueñas*. He knows versions of all the major styles but it's in the *malagueña* where he fully pours out his personal expression. The *malagueña* that is always inside of me is Diego "El Pijín," sitting in a chair, leaning in towards the guitar, making that deep delicate opening line, his eyes almost closed, sitting in his own country of silence while the guitar rises and falls on its sea of sound, stops, and then Diego enters the song like a ship quietly leaving the harbor.

2

Yo soy como aquel navío
cuando lo están carenando
mientras más golpes le dan
más firme se va queando.

I'm like that ship
Put in for repairs
The more blows they give it
The firmer it remains.

*A*t the time I entered the world of flamenco,
I was living in Fuengirola, a small coastal village in the throes of
transition from a poor, ugly fishing town to a thriving, ugly resort.
The two experiences were intertwined, both inside me and in their
own convolutions. Both were a springboard for meditation on myself in relation to that singular circus we call society.

I had come to Málaga from New York with Joan, an American
Negro girl of West Indian parentage. In Fuengirola I began to move
between the peace of the countryside and the world of flamenco.
At first Joan enjoyed the Peña. She liked the music, the atmosphere,

the new friends. But eventually, flamenco palls if you don't participate either by singing or playing or through speech and *palmas*. And though Joan liked the sounds, there was no dance. Without dance, fête for her was just not fête. Finally, the long hours of sitting and listening to the talk and the songs were too passive for Joan. After a while, she stayed at home in Fuengirola and I went to the Peña by myself.

Joan did not take part in my country wandering. She was essentially a city girl. The country was all right as a lark, but she needed her drink, her music, her bar and another, more urban conversation. In New York this was fine. It's what was. And it's what I was. In New York, within the rhythms of our passionate first love, in my Bleecker Street loft, we plunged and floated to Bach, Bird, Miles, Vivaldi, Sparrow, Melody, rum-and-cheese omelets. Amid the family of mice that came up through the rotting wooden floor, around the altar of our pot-belly stove, we danced our love dance and made our own world against that alien one out there. But in Andalusia it was different. Here was a reality I didn't want to ignore, I wanted to take part in it. I was in a state of unrest, confusion and sterility that preceded the opening into "a larger life." The *campo* and the world of flamenco were catalysts of this change in me. Joan retreated from both. In the spring of '61, after the two years we'd spent together in a modern apartment on the beach, Joan went back to the United States and I moved three miles up to an abandoned cottage at the foot of the sierra, where I was to live for the next two and a half years.

I was sick of the forces that were changing the Andalusian coast into a Miami Beach, I was broke, the view and the area were beautiful. My cottage was a kilometer from the road, there was no electricity and I had to carry water from a well about fifty yards steeply below. The sea, sky, clouds, and landscape were in the house as I wrote, ate, or read by the open door. I taught the neighboring farm children reading, writing, and arithmetic. For pay I received vegetables, fruit, oil, eggs, bread, and whatever the season brought. I was never hungry; I had all the material comforts I needed. I didn't need money in the hills. Whatever my twin sister, Elaine, who was my Theodore Van Gogh, sent me, was spent in town or in Málaga when I went to the Peña. Living in the hills was very different from what I had imagined and at thirty-three I found myself with a new set of ABC's. They had to do with silence, with space, with the elements, with nature, with being alone. And being with people who made their life from the land without the aid of machines. Precisely the phenomena absent or mutilated in Brooklyn where I was born. Precisely the phenomena that are roots and humus of flamenco.

I looked at my neighbors. Those below me, closer to the highway and to town, moved around on bicycles and motorcycles, copied the latest fashions, were curious about the tourists, and, though certain attitudes and superstitions were of another century, they were definitely living in this one. One rhythm of modernity is the shift from rural to urban life. And these people were swept into the fever of the current dream: that of selling the farm to a rich foreigner for a fabulous amount and then going to live in town. Above me, up in the sierra, the people moved around on mules or burros, they were not poorer, but their houses, clothes, furniture, attitudes, and daily rhythms were of the past century. The machine was something they saw pass on the road, down there. Up in the hills there were only goat paths. The people went to town to sell their produce and on feast days. Their life was connected to the land. And they were still making Diego's sound. It was not as polished, as nuanced; it was not flamenco, but it was the same sound historically. They sang when they threshed and when they carted goods. The people below me were still *andaluz* but sang the latest popular ballads—Italian, American, Spanish—which all had one thing in common: silence and space had been removed from the sound. And although I made valuable research in libraries, heard hundreds of records, and went to many live sessions, without the experience in the hills, the study would have been only partial. In the late nineteenth century, flamenco's high point, the *andaluz* fused plural racial influences into a superb poetry and music. The flamenco sound rises from the sierra, the hot plain, the coast, the riverbank, the plowed fields, enters the towns and cities, is transformed by artists whose roots are rural, and pierces the heart of the poet. In the twentieth century the impetus is reversed. The poet and the thinker create institutions, sometimes vital, to revive, encourage, and nourish the singer. Flamenco survives—in homes, taverns, inns, anywhere a certain breed of Andalusians come together, drink wine and when their blood begins to hum, they must sing and listen to flamenco in order to elaborate the emotional impulse. The flamenco resists but the movement of history is to place him on a reservation.

That first night at the Peña I met a short, chunky, beak-nosed dynamo of a man called Manolo, "El Herraor," The Blacksmith. The word "met" is ridiculously inadequate when applied to Manolillo. He entered my life so fully that now, seven years later, whenever I go to Málaga I look around for him on the known corners, in the bars, hoping I'll run into him because he is always a warm, desired prologue to any of the later rhythms. But he's like that with everyone. I've seen him with people who speak no Spanish and he always breaks through to them. Manolo is a prototype of the *andaluz* in maximum vitality: vehement talker, pungent joke-teller, master of mime and anecdote. He is an anarchist who needs people. He would die not from hunger or thirst but from lack of sympathetic people to respond to his personal repertory. With him, the curtain is always up on a vaudeville show where everything is a little larger than life size. He himself is not exaggerated because he is so real. You tell him your sorrow and you see him nodding and clucking, and right away he chews up your pain into his own system and starts telling you one of his million anecdotes all swollen with how courageous he was, how much suffering he endured, and maybe there's a sudden erotic turn in the story and suddenly you're laughing at the exaggeration and your own pain fades away as Manolo nourishes you with his own humanity. His esthetic sensibility is always linked to what is tangibly human. His verbal art is never merely stylistic. If his imagination flies it always carries the beating heart with it.

Of all the intimate friendships I made with the flamencos of Málaga, it's revealing that Manolo came to my house most often. He is hungry for new worlds and to come to my house in Fuengirola was to make a voyage abroad. There were always food and drink, music, and once in a while, attractive women. This last item turned him into such a bantam rooster that I could hear the crowing in his glances. Someone would say, "Let's go for a swim," and if there was a good-looking woman around, Manolo had his trunks on and was moving toward the beach before I was out of the chair. When he got back he would lean in confidentially and say: "What a pair of thighs. She must be great in the bed, huh?" Manolo always assumed I had made love to all the women I introduced him to, partly to con me, partly because he knew he was talking to a fellow voluptuary, and partly to light the incense for a story about his own fabulous sexual prowess. I would say: "Come on, Manolo, you're sixty-two." It was as if I'd accidentally knocked over his wine. He'd step back so as not to get wet, make a joke, fill the glass again, and pick up where he'd left off. When I moved up into the hills he also visited me. But it was different. This was no new world: he'd spent fifty years shoeing animals all over the province. It was quiet and peaceful: too peaceful, and he was restless for a larger audience. Unlike Diego, the bigger the audience, the more worlds to feed his appetite for life.

Manolo embodies the idea that the singer sings those styles that express his way of being. And since he ranges from the harsh realist to the tender sentimentalist, from the eternal rebel to the pragmatist, he has found three styles that he sings with personal vibration: the tango of "El Piyayo," the *martinete*, and the *guajira*.

Rafael Flores Nieto, nicknamed "El Piyayo," was a gypsy from Málaga who lived roughly between 1870 and a few years after the Spanish Civil War. His family were smiths and horsedealers. He was an adventurer, fought in the Spanish-American and the Moroccan wars, and later in life strapped a battered guitar to his back, carried a box of ribbons, socks, and odds and ends, and wandered from café to café playing and singing his tango, which is a flamenco tango from Cádiz and bears no relation to the Argentine *tango*. The *tango* of "El Piyayo" is an interesting potpourri because it contains fragments of the *carcelera*, a jailhouse song similar to the *martinete*, as well as the *guajira*, a Cuban song transformed into the flamenco genre. "El Piyayo" was the last of the Andalusian wandering minstrels, and his great talent was an ability to improvise a poetry that contains just about every type of attitude and feeling. Like all singers, he borrowed from the anonymous

17

songbook but most of the poems have his own personal stamp. Manolo, born in 1900, was always in contact with the gypsy smiths and stock-dealers, and he lived many years in close friendship with "El Piyayo." In Málaga he is his leading, and perhaps last, disciple, knows hundreds of his songs, and sings them with a lilting, picaresque grace like no one else:

Tú eres lo mismo que el cuco
pájaro que nunca anida
pone el huevo en nido ajeno
y otro pájaro lo cría.

You're just like the cuckoo
Bird that never nests
She lays an egg in another's nest
The other bird must raise it.

The tango of "El Piyayo" fits Manolillo to a T. For one thing there is a good deal of the bard in him, and those songs that deal with war and tell about bloody battles, valiant generals, tropical fruits, and sweet offerings of the Cuban women permit Manolo to declaim his own vision of history. It's not enough that he's a *cantaor*: he wants to be professor, poet, historian, politician, lover, actor, world traveler. He wants to be *everything*. His didactic strokes are beautiful because they are always suffused with *gracia*[1]. Manolo is a walking bundle of *gracia*.

Even if you placed Manolo in another country, he would be a *pícaro*. He has the physical looks, the wit, the rascally charm, the obscenity, the cunning and endurance to survive, the loyalty that changes according to how he is treated. When Manolo sings the tango of "El Piyayo" he *is* it. But it's hard to understand this without actually seeing and hearing him. Ideally, this book should be accompanied by a few choice records by Diego, Manolo, and the singers to come. Better yet, it should be followed by a documentary film. But anyway, the tango of Cádiz has a sliding, infectious beat, made for dance, and was the traditional music for the witty, satirical

[1] The word *gracia* is one of the most difficult to translate. Though it often involves verbal play, it may also be in a gesture such as raising the arms in dance, in a way of walking, or in a tiny thing like a glance. It includes more than charm or grace or wit. *Gracia* stems from the animated and joyful heart.

comparsas of pre-Civil War fame, where everyone and everything was mocked but with such a bite that the musicians often ended up in jail. Which brings us to another branch of "El Piyayo's" poems: once again, Manolo, having fought with the Republic and having spent time in prison, spills out jailhouse songs, but in "El Piyayo's" idiom they are always tempered with a clowning, shrugging tone that is perfect for Manolo because he can never stay angry too long:

> *Al juez que me sentenció*
> *le tengo que regalar*
> *las balas de mi pistola*
> *cuando salga en libertad.*

> To the judge who sentenced me
> I must make a gift
> Of the bullets of my pistol
> The day they set me free.

> *Las cárceles son iglesias*
> *los presidiarios los santos*
> *y los cabos los faroles*
> *que alumbran² de cuando en cuando.*

> Jails are churches
> The prisoners are the saints
> And the turnkeys are the lanterns
> That light up from time to time.

In the erotic poems of "El Piyayo," the richest theme in the flamenco songbook, Manolo pours out all the dramatic sentimentality of his being. In Andalusia, Eros suffers frustration. Woman is inaccessible as woman; only as wife and mother does she deliver herself. The theme resounds through the flamenco *coplas*:

> *Compañerita del alma*
> *qué pena pasa aquel*
> *que tiene el agua en los labios*
> *y no la puede beber.³*

² *Alumbran* is used here as a double-entendre, meaning also "they beat up."

³ This is a regular *copla flamenca* and not one of "El Piyayo's" songs. For other *coplas* dealing with the theme of sexual frustration, see the list in the appendix.

> Companion of my soul
> What sorrow feels he
> Who has water at his lips
> And cannot drink it.

"El Piyayo" speaks differently about love. He expresses either a joyous adoration or a bitter hatred uttered with terrible directness:

> *La tierra que a mí me cubra*
> *ni la mires ni la pises*
> *no te acuerdas más de mí*
> *que mi nombre te maldice*
> *muerto reniego de ti.*

> The earth that covers me
> Don't look at it or step on it
> Don't remember me
> For my name curses you
> And dead, I disown you.

> *Hermosa mía no me llores*
> *que ya me tienes tú aquí*
> *cuando te vi de venir*
> *por el jardín de las flores*
> *de alegría que me entró*
> *cantaron los ruiseñores.*

> My lovely one don't cry
> For now I'm here
> When I saw you come
> Through the garden of flowers
> From the joy that pierced me
> The nightingales began to sing.

With his head cocked to one side, and ending with a grin, Manolo loves to sing those songs that have delicate floral imagery, and then maybe a few minutes later this lyrical Spanish Cagney enters the dark precincts of the *martinete*, the song of the forge.

Singers lean toward the styles that are intimate vehicles for their manner of being, but the quality of the voice is also an important factor. A melodious tenor is not apt for the songs of the forge, which require, rather, a harsh, hoarse, aphonic voice. If a tenor sings them well and with feeling, he may provoke an *ole*, but something is missing and that something is the sound of the forge itself. In the same way, a singer with a harsh voice is deficient in most styles of the *malagueña*, which need a delicate, melodious rendition. The subtle variety of hoarse voices creates a richness of emotional textures: there is the voice that lashes with virile defiance, another that has a sad accent of resignation, another that has almost extra-human sounds so wrought with anguish it is the wound that sings; there is a hoarseness that is metallic and another that is actually lyrical. Manolo's hoarseness, called *rajo* in Spanish, is "lyrical" in the tango of "El Piyayo" but something else in the *martinete*. Then there are strange nuances in female hoarseness— what is called a "gypsy echo." "La Fernanda de Utrera" has an echo so tribal that if you close your eyes you are at a campfire in some vacant lot and no other world exists. "La Niña de los Peines" has more physical resources, more melody—her echo is sonorous and almost wholesome; you shake your head in admiration and smile, but with "La Fernanda" there is more shadow and more pain.

The trades of farrier and smith are classical with the gypsy, who has always been the great interpreter of the *martinete*. The *martinete* belongs to those primitive songs called *cante jondo* and is sung without guitar accompaniment. Most of the verses deal with jailhouse themes, trials and personal tribulations and the defiance of the race. There is always the feeling of the cave, the closed door, of anguish choked to a half-voice so the law cannot hear. All this and more is heard when Manolo sings. *Martinete* also means hammer, and after fifty years of wielding it, all the echoes, strokes, and silences have crept into his voice. He is getting older now and both the hammer and the song are a terrible strain:

> *Estoy en mi calabozo*
> *me meten en otro más malo*
> *tan oscuro que no veía*
> *ni los deítos de la mano.*

> I'm in my cell
> They put me in one worse
> So dark I couldn't see
> The fingers of my hand.

21

With the *guajira*, a Cuban folk song transformed into the flamenco genre at the turn of the century, Manolo reverts to his lyrical vein, but now the air is filled with the smell of ripe pineapple, coconut, sugar cane, with swaying, sensual Cuban women. In Manolo's throat the women are always just about to surrender, the breeze is always a caress, the cigar is just about to be lit, the rich coffee is sipped. The *guajira* in its melody has a tendency toward sweetness. The "operatic" singer, the virtuoso warbler, makes it saccharine. Manolo's hoarse voice, short breath-line, and salty delivery result in a spicy blend that avoids sentimentality.

A singer like Manolo defies all the rules, the limiting definitions. It always happens in flamenco. The intellectuals make rules and then a singer comes along, opens his mouth, and says *ay*! in a particular way and the rules come tumbling down. Manolo has very limited physical resources. He cannot maintain the long, extended line of many flamenco styles. But his *human* resources are rich and they are what create the emotion. He struggles with the *martinete*, fighting to get each note out full and vibrant—the form of the song already there because the fifty years in the forge have entered his voice and still he struggles each time he sings it—that is his essential magic and the magic of flamenco.

Unlike Diego, Manolillo talks readily and endlessly about the past. But you can't force him; some natural association in the conversation must prepare the terrain. At first I took his historical references literally. Since all flamencos are passionately involved with personal idols, they are prolific legend-makers, and Manolo is no exception. He out-invents all of them. But confusion set in after I'd heard different versions from others. I went back to check them out with him. He just stood there, head tilted back, hand on hip, and he looked at me. His look said two things. One: whose word are you going to take, mine or some idiot's who wasn't there, and two: even if I *did* exaggerate a little, what do you want, some dull prosaic account or my more artistic version? I never questioned him again. Here and there, in moments of fatigue and pain, he puts aside dramatic exaggeration and a plainer, quieter fact slips in. But I prefer the dramatic invention and Manolo knows it.

At any rate, through him I get a pulsing picture of Málaga throughout the century, not only the flamenco scene but also a vision of the social dynamics, because Manolo, as a flamenco and as a smith, had direct intercourse with all levels. He has heard all the great singers from 1915 to the present but the great years for him are those up to the Civil War. In those years he was in his prime, there was an abundance of spontaneous sessions and of great *aficionados*, and he was an active participant. He traveled all over Andalusia and went to all the stock fairs. He practiced veterinary work illegally, and often advised landowner friends on purchases of horses and mules. Diego reveals very little about the professional scene of his day, but Manolo spills over with stories of the semiprofessional atmosphere, the picaresque day-to-day struggle to eat, the all-night brawls. In 1930 he was a leading figure in the Blacksmith's Union and he is terribly proud of his craft. He says: "I emancipated myself in the year so and so," meaning he stopped working for someone else and set up his own shop. He is so fiercely wonderfully socialistic, without abstract theories, and a great part of his life was killed when *he* lost the war, though now and again pre-war memories flame up in him. One night, high from the wine and the singing, walking home from a session with me and Pepe Luque, the lawyer—who was born into the leisure class and has exactly the opposite politics—Manolo declaimed in a loud voice in the square of the Cathedral of Málaga, opposite the Bishop's Palace: "It's so simple. A man has five thousand acres. He doesn't need all that land. You leave him what he needs and you distribute the rest among those who have nothing. It's simple, isn't it?" We laughed because of the way he said it but it was more than funny. Bertolt Brecht couldn't have said it any better.

Manolo has been through the mill. He can be an angry man but there's no bitterness in him. He's sixty-seven now; his trade is finished; he works in a silo sewing up bags of wheat. This gives him his miserable daily wage, will provide for social security and his old-age pension. But his appetite for life is unabated. I see him confronting new situations, new people, and there's always some new color, some new texture I hadn't noticed before. He's a mountain stream that never dries up. Manolo *is* Spain with all its peculiar paradoxes. He's harsh and tender at the same time, a salty rogue with a profound sense of courtesy and dignity for himself and for others; they're beating him on the head all the time but he still comes up singing. A vision of Spain that shows only the sinister, the sorrow, the defeat, the lament, is fragmentary at best, as is the "tambourine" vision—the castanets, the merry, picturesque, poster focus. Lament and laughter flow into the same mold. The only thing we have close to it is the blues.

Manolo. It's raining in the hills now and I'm thinking: if it lets up, I'll go down, catch the train, and try and find him.

3

Tengo momentos en la noche
cuando la muerte me apetecía
si Dios no me la manda
es que no la merecería.

I have moments in the night
When I'm hungry for death
If God doesn't send it to me
It's because I don't deserve it.

*O*n Saturday nights I made the twenty-mile run from Fuengirola to Málaga on the diesel-engine "Toonerville trolley" that ran parallel to the sea. I went alone or with Joan, whose musically parched West Indian soul found an oasis in the live singing at the Peña. Though I'm sure if a steel band had ever hit Málaga, she would have deserted me and the flamencos with a joyous movement of her supple hips. We were treated with extra warmth as though we were two strange birds dragged in out of a storm who unexpectedly turned out to be charming and, finally, not so strange. I spoke Spanish well and would have been a monster not to respond openly to such friendliness, and Joan was the only woman among men who were very conscious of the feminine emanations she sent out in the smoke-filled tiny room of Casa Luna. She was the Antillean woman of Manolo's songs, the warm caress of a Caribbean breeze, the ripe tropical fruit. And Manolo, whenever he sang the *guajira*, sang it for her and to her.

That first year there was a tremendous intimacy in the Peña: only six to twelve members, save for an exceptional evening when it might mount to twenty. In the beginning I was so eager to learn everything at once that I was impatient at talk that touched any other theme. It took me a while to learn that the true flamenco cannot enter a room, sit down, open his mouth, and begin to sing. I was imposing my rational intensity and a compulsive city sense of time on an expression that has its own rhythms of birth and silence. But one evening I paid my dues. It was in the middle of a good session, everyone mellow and the singing deep and moving. An intruder interrupted the flow, and, trying to revive it, I thought I'd draw Diego out by asking him about some poem. He recited it to me and I said, "No, sing it." He replied, "Quiet, stupid." I blinked, but I had to swallow it. He was telling me: "In the first place, who do you think you're fooling? And second: I sing when I feel like it. You just sit there, take another sip of wine, and wait. There are no faucets here that turn on feelings instantaneously. I have to go to a well and it takes a little time. All you have to do is listen but I have to make the sound." Though all music involves the feelings, flamenco has the added dimension of a physical complexity and strain that can lead to absurdity. There is a double vulnerability: one physical and the other emotional. It's not enough to render a style with technical accuracy: the singer who does not move you has failed. This is a tremendous burden and therefore slower preparatory rhythms must precede the fuller, deeper release.

Thirty years of New York living had made me a slave to time like the rest of my compatriots. I had to learn to endure *actively* within time, to ignore clock time, to forget tomorrow so as not to kill off the potential of now. The flamenco uses time as a substance in which he unfolds his feelings and within which he spends himself. Time is subservient to his reality and not vice versa. If the moment is rich he keeps it going. If the moment is poor he sticks it out until something better is forged. Tomorrow is confronted tomorrow. Living in the hills helped me to understand this. The actual relinquishing of the sense of time I was born into is another thing. But I'm working on it. The flamencos of Málaga flattered me by exaggerating my knowledge, telling me how remarkable it was that an American loved and understood their music. But it was my *intuition* of certain psychological norms and taboos that made them accept me, if not as a flamenco, not being *andaluz*, then as a passionate lover of their *manner of being*, and as someone a little strange who somehow fitted.

The solid intimacy, the healthy teasing, the rich variety of laughter, the astonishing reality of a group of men, all distinct individuals, who came together to spend Saturday nights singing and listening to singing—it was a fountain I had to return to. I think if I had not stumbled onto the Peña and the world of flamenco, I would have left the Costa del Sol. The conversion of Fuengirola to a modern seaside resort horror was getting to me. The rotting ancient values were being quickly replaced by new, shiny money-colored ones—the same ones I had fled three thousand miles to escape. Unbelievable sums of money were changing hands, and everyone, from the mayor to the sorriest beggar, wanted to get in on it. The general greed was making them deaf and blind to every-thing except the sound and sight of money. But I was deafer and even more blind. I expected people to sing and there was no singing in Fuengirola. Men bewildered by change don't sing. Those who usher in and become leaders of the change don't sing. They have more important occupations: they buy and sell land and build bungalows, beauty parlors, bowling alleys, barbecue joints, bars, and curio shops.

But my secret rage was that they treated me the same as the other foreigners. I spoke to them in perfect Spanish; they answered me in pidgin language. In the midst of the bewilderment and the greed fevers I expected them to distinguish; I expected them to see I was different, that I was a passionate student of their country I refused to accept the change. I tried to remain aloof, walk in the country, stay in the house, avoid the town—but it was absurd. The change was there in the very air, in the growing garbage heaps. I too was infected: I became petty, defensive, quarrelsome; I imagined everybody was out to cheat me. The truth is I was living a *little* life. The days consisted in pleasing and sating the belly, the sexual impulse, the need for fantasy, and, above all, in maintaining a sense of superiority over everyone—the tourists, the foreign residents, the townsmen. This could be done only through a cunning evasion of self. Wine was fifteen cents a liter and with a hundred pesetas ($1.65) in my pocket I felt rich. I pretended Málaga was still a semi-utopia and from my thirty-dollars-a-month sunlit chalet I wrote poems about the landscape.

The men of the Peña were different. They were not hicks awed by change. One has only to go into Málaga today, in the height of the Costa del Sol development, to perceive the difference. Fuengirola and Torremolinos are completely new towns. Málaga has been able to absorb the change with more grace. Its architectural face has not been deformed. But more important, the men of the Peña were not caught up in the general fever of greed or in the accelerated rhythms. They were conscious of the change; it touched their lives—who hasn't wistfully dreamed of getting rich quick— but they were not *bewildered*. During the week they performed their various jobs as waiter, lawyer, blacksmith, mason, electrician, railroad worker, archivist, and on Saturday nights they came together for the desired ritual of *cante*. The music was the marrow, but equally important was the sharing of passion, the being part of a group that nourished each person who had something to give —even if it was just being a good listener. The Peña was a society more satisfactory than that other one they struggled and lived in during the rest of the week. To enter the little room where the sessions were held was to leave that world behind and become enveloped in a new one: a desired one. It was a sanctuary but with certain norms: the pseudo-*aficionados* were quickly weeded out. There was wine, song, humor, and intimacy. There were also envies, disputes, petty gossip, but they never threatened the central structure. The cost of the wine was shared by the members. It was two months before they let me pay.

With Diego in the hospital the singers were reduced to Manolo, a few good *aficionados*, and an occasional unknown who might spark the session for a night. But as far as I was concerned, no one could take Diego's place—until Manolo brought a thin, dark, intense-looking man who stunned us that first night and on many others: Ángel Luiggi.

Ángel has a weeping, sobbing quality in his voice along with a high-pitched, defiant anguish—the anguish of a man who was destined to be nothing else but a flamenco singer but who, through circumstance, bad luck, damage to his vocal chords, inadequacy, never made it the way he wanted to, as a successful professional. But *cante*, in any form, is his life and so every time he sings, he sings against his fate. This is what creates the emotion. No singer is able to sing with profound feeling every time. But when Ángel has been singing for an hour or two without really exposing the deep wounds, sometimes the days of bitterness mount into one moment and he stops feinting and parrying with his voice and brings it up fully from way inside: the difference has a texture like a clay you could shape.

The world of flamenco abounds with singers like Ángel who want to be pros, actually have some early success, and then through strain or limitation discover they have only partial strength in their voice or lungs. Obsessed with fear of failure, they lack the confidence to perform night after night before strange audiences. Although they earn money from time to time at spontaneous private fiestas, they make a living at something else. They are a classical type of listening *aficionado*, often paying money to other singers, whether they themselves are down and out or successful. For Ángel, *cante* is the one area in which he can momentarily transcend the defeats of daily life. He is too proud to work steadily for someone else, so in the spring, summer, and early autumn he works the fairs all over Andalusia as a waiter. At the fairs he often picks up extra money by singing, but more important, he lives as a flamenco rebelling against control from outside and refusing to be a slave to time. He works hard for a few weeks, then lays off according to what he earns. And he supports a wife and five kids. There is no one motive that shapes a *cantaor*, but I like to think that with Ángel pride coupled to a real social bitterness is one of the major factors in his sound of weeping anguish that is sometimes defiant, sometimes just weeping, but always pure lament.

Ángel came that first night and most of the members did not

know him. He was silent, gypsy looking, very dapper, aloof, and removed. He was the opposite of Manolillo: he did not give himself easily. But when he sang, two terms that the flamencos use became realities: one is "to fight with the song" and the other is "to sing with feeling." But I was not ready for the full impact of Ángel's singing. It's one thing to sit in a cabaret and listen to a singer on the stage and another for him to sing directly to you. Often, after the session broke up at Casa Luna, the remaining "pillars" would find another bar, and there, standing up, Manolillo and Ángel would continue. One night, Ángel put his arm around me and sang right into my face. I was so embarrassed I barely heard what he was singing. I had become a part of the singer's struggle. He was singing to *me* and he was waiting for a response. I had never before encountered an artistic form where the witness was immediately morally and emotionally involved in the artist's expression and *had to tell him directly right then and there*. I just wasn't ready for it, and I realized that too often in the past I had fled or frozen in similar experiences. I was uneasy while Ángel was singing to me and I faked a reaction. Ángel knew it and he turned away from me. Much later, after living and learning in the world of flamenco, I lost some of the fear and was able to react truthfully. I knew this by the look on Ángel's face. One night, when he himself couldn't reach inside, I let him know this by *silence*, and he didn't turn from me. He just as silently acknowledged my response. It's fantastic how the authentic flamenco can pick up the tiniest false gesture. If I am obsessed with this essential flamenco norm it's because, during the same period, I was getting ready to assess a life of self-deceit and cowardice. The structure of flamenco acted as a catalyst and provided foundations for a new start.

Ángel opened up new dimensions for me in the world of *cante*. Because he is a city boy he gave me an insight into the urban singer and the urban style of the *fandanguillo*. In the last two generations the urban dimensions of Andalusia have grown considerably, and this naturally affects flamenco. I saw it clearly in the contrast between Manolo and Ángel. Manolo, sixty-seven, was born in the capital, but with his trade, his weather-beaten face, his stance, and the fact that in his youth Málaga was really just a large, provincial farming and fishing town, he is really only half urban, or urban of fifty years ago, which is a huge difference. Ángel, forty-nine, was actually born in Álora and came to Málaga as a young boy. His humor, his dress, his way of approaching you, his con-man's verbal play—all smell of a crowded apartment in a poor neighborhood. If you picked Ángel up and placed him on the corner of Forty-second Street and Broadway, he would be a part of the scene. Although Ángel is not more or less flamenco than Manolo, his manner of expression is affected by this basic difference. The verses of his *fandanguillos* deal with prostitution, crime, sexual betrayal, social injustice. Manolo's *tangos* are about lyrical love, rural scenes, military adventures, the jailhouse, with a picaresque country wit running through them. Both styles are flamenco; both stem from a huge sensitivity to the human tragicomedy. But by the time the *fandanguillo* reached Ángel, it had already entered its phase of mass entertainment, of "operatic" interpreters, of vulgarity, both in the verse and the musical innovations. But there have been several excellent stylists of the *fandanguillo* who through their personal depth as singers were able to give it a certain grandeur, and Ángel had the good taste to imitate their versions.

It took me a long time to savor the urban accent, the modern transitions and innovations. It took me a long time to be receptive to sounds other than Diego's. I was doing what the vast majority of *aficionados* do: we limit flamenco to the small area of our tastes and perceptions. But, slowly, the force of this other manner of being imposed itself and unlocked certain prejudices and broadened my historical vision of what has happened and what is happening in Spain. My life-long dissatisfaction with contemporary society set up a resistance to the positive expressions that exist in it. As to other worlds I came to flamenco with the conviction that it was a thing of the past. Then I discovered that it was the expression of a particular way of living life, very different from that of my countrymen, and very much alive. This whole book is nothing but an attempt to describe that way of life and how it affected me.

We organized a recording session. We set the date and the hour very seriously. And almost everyone showed up. But being flamencos, the planning was loose: the small detail of the guitarist had somehow slipped by and our last-minute search was fruitless. All the guitars in Málaga were either in the Torremolinos night clubs or out of town. Diego, who had been mellow and flowing at midday, suddenly shied away from us. We thought we might tape some of the songs that didn't have guitar accompaniment but he refused to come. A gloom fell over us, but we went through the motions and walked over to Ángel's house where the session was to take place. When we got there we found his little girl sick with the measles. It looked like the session was out. Ángel's wife insisted we sit down. Wine was sent for and the idea was to have a quick drink and then depart. We were Pepe Luque, the lawyer; his sister; me; Danny Swerdloff, an American painter; Manolo; and Ángel and his family. We sat in the small living room, joked and talked, two more bottles of wine were sent for, and some quiet presence entered all of us.

We had never sat like this before, talking in a particular, casual intimacy, easily liking one another. Usually the singing was the powerful dominant character, but not this night. Ángel showed us some old photos taken when he was twenty, and I was startled to see the beautiful, sensitive face of a child. After about an hour and a half, really thinking there was to be no singing that night— and maybe that was the difference—there was no pressure of *having to sing*, and this created a languorous, easy-going atmosphere—one of Ángel's sons, a boy of twelve, was half coaxed into singing. Half coaxed, because he really did want to sing and once he got rid of his nervousness we couldn't stop him. He was great. Although his voice was not yet formed and was too young for the physical and technical complexities, he had a feeling for the music and was able to make the flamenco sound. His trying was enough to move us because even though he couldn't finish the songs properly, for lack of breath, it didn't matter. While he was singing, the father said to him: "Pull it towards the inside!" Meaning that the sound has to go from the throat to the interior and then be released. The boy imitated Ángel's style and gestures and the father tried to make a sophisticated, knowing grin but it came out tender. Then, still a little nervous, the boy stood in profile and began singing the tango of "El Piyayo." He calls them "Manolillo's songs" because he's only heard them from Manolo and it was beautiful to see the red-faced blacksmith, his hands on the boy's arms, nodding and smiling, encouraging him. Danny and I looked at each other: now he understood what I meant about flamenco being a living form. We were in the pulsing middle of it in Ángel's house. The flame was passed on from father to son and Manolo, the disciple of "El Piyayo," now had his own disciple. The boy really had a salty grace perfect for these songs. Then the older son tried to sing, but he was scared and the sound came out too controlled and from the surface. Ángel called it "cowardly *cante*," meaning that he was singing from the throat only. I learned more in that moment than I had in listening to a host of professional singers. The younger boy lacked fullness of voice and lungs but his *struggle* carried him through to emotive moments. The older boy, unable to loosen the knot of fear, was making pretty sounds but they were not flamenco sounds. I understood then that only the singer who dares to expose and risk himself, physically and emotionally, can make the flamenco sound.

Then Ángel started singing. It was his moment, he was proud of his son, and the sweetness of the gathering stirred him. Guitars, tape recorders, time, all were forgotten. He sang a gamut of his most emotive *fandanguillos*. He sang *por soleares* and *siguiriyas*. He even entered Manolo's kingdom and sang "El Piyayo" and the *martinete*. The session broke up early only because the sick child needed sleep. As we left I had to tell them what they were all feeling: "What a delicious session and you know why? Because it was so tender. It was the way you should make love to a woman." This last with a smile and a glance at Pepe Luque's sister. But it was true. Who knows what other mood it might have passed into if it had continued. But there had been no straining, no competing, no envy or "prima donna-ism" that usually mark other sessions. And the family thing in it, not cloying or making Junior recite, was natural and desired. If the tourists could be part of such an evening for one hour. . . . For one thing, it would put the tourist agencies out of business. It would be an immersion in a real stream and not the prettified swimming pool set up next to the sea.

What amazes me about Ángel is seeing the multiple ways he expresses himself. Most people have a wide range of emotions but they have limited vocal devices and gestures for communicating. Angel can be expansive, tight lipped, bragging, modest (this not very often), merry, bitter, sardonic, wisecracking, obscene, hard, tender, removed, giving, angry, bored, satirical, sentimental, and his genius is that he always finds the perfect vocal vessel in which to project the moment's particular feeling. Like Manolo he is an oral magician, but he is more ambitious than Manolo. He is a great tease and pokes fun at me, an American involved with flamenco. With a straight face he says: "Listen Pablo, take me with you to America. We'll go to Washington and we'll say to your President: How come you're spending so much money and energy making atomic bombs when what the world really needs is a new *fandango*? Then we'll set up an academy in the White House, teach them flamenco and make a pile of money, okay?" Twenty seconds later he's in the middle of a weeping lament, making you feel it; he finishes, sees the effect on your face, and comes out with a Donald Duck-voiced wisecrack. Angel is a smoldering incarnation of the Andalusian manner that mixes tragedy with spoof and satire. He loves to puncture people who puff themselves up with their own importance. Yet he himself has a gigantic ego. I doubt whether he has "a good heart," but he definitely has a passionate one. Angel's bitterness and envy are a double-edged sword. It creates the anguish of his expression but it destroys his personal relationships. Nothing can be done about it. He is consumed by the desire to be a "successful" artist, and since he hasn't achieved it, he's a bitter critic of all others. I tried to tell him once that it didn't matter. We were at a session where I was paying more attention to a newcomer. He came over to me and whispered in my ear: "I'm surprised at you, Pablo. He's not much of a singer." I told him to forget about knocking other singers. He exploded his envy in my face and for the rest of the evening I was busy picking out the shrapnel.

Angel taught me by his *being* that what marks the true flamenco is a total spending of himself without calculation. What ends a session is that there is nothing more to say that night. But when there is a lull, or the bar closes up and we go out into the street, apparently each to his own bed, when we think there is nothing more to say, then someone who all night has been trying to get at something locked away where we hide things from ourselves and from other men, someone starts singing again. And then only physical exhaustion will end it. My first thought that this was some new race with special powers of endurance finally ripened into an awareness that they only seemed so because they are able to cast aside the controls we usually carry in the company of others. The flamenco abandons himself, not in Dionysian frenzy toward oblivion, but through traditional ritual. There he lets out his own drama, which is also the drama of many men. This is what I had wanted to be able to do as a writer, but it had been bottled up for so many years because I was overly concerned with the word as form rather than as an apt vessel for the inner drama that was constantly going on. The authentic flamenco singer learns the traditional forms but is not imprisoned in their structure. They are the well-made instruments which must then be played by someone with a creative flame who makes a sound that stirs us. All those years I was mired in beautiful swamps of words but I was saying nothing. Nothing about what was really happening to me. I thought that creativity was to make something original, something un-known, some new alignment of words never uttered before that somehow magically would reach the sensitive reader. I knew I was suffering, loving, hating, reacting intensely to life within and around me. It never occurred to me that, being different to begin with, all I had to do was to tell the story of my life, of my drama, in my own words. What a shock to sit next to Ángel and listen to some other singer with a powerful voice intricately playing with the structure of a style and then afterwards to have Ángel turn to me and say: "Nothing—he isn't saying a thing." Because it was true. No one had felt a thing because the singer himself felt nothing but was merely making surface sounds. You don't have to know flamenco to perceive this. Somehow a man who is merely declaim-ing a song is transparent to all. It's true, there are also those sing-ers who do feel the song, who do want to communicate an emotion, but who, through some psychic fault, some fear, some expressive door they can't unlock, fail to do so. Here a knowledge of flamenco helps. But what is also true is that there are those singers short on voice modulation, melodic intricacy, lung power, technical or virtuoso adornments, but whose sound, coming straight from the center of intense feeling, penetrates immediately and powerfully. This is what happened, to a lesser degree, when Ángel's boy sang. We are so wrapped up in the abstractions and the divinities of the meaning of art that often this pure, felt sound does not touch us. But the flamencos are not fooled. So-and-so may be earning fantastic sums in the latest club, but when they want to hear real singing they gather in some quiet corner and listen to the "unknown" *cantaor*. Ángel is a success; it's the accessories that obsess and destroy him. His tragedy is that he doesn't know it.

4

Presumes que eres la ciencia
y yo no lo entiendo así
cómo siendo tú la ciencia
no habías comprendió a mí.

You say you're science
And I just don't see it that way
How can you be science
When you haven't understood me.

*D*iego, Manolillo, and Ángel are not great singers. All three lack the complex physical requirements. Manolo and Ángel have limited repertories[1] and Diego has only a thread of sound left. But they have something which is rare and which always excites me: their sound is that of "men of one piece." Though they sing someone else's songs,[2] the songs become *theirs*.

[1] Since the original writing, Ángel, tremendous *aficionado* that he is, has increased his repertory and now sings more completely and more emotionally such major styles as the *solea*, the *siguiriya*, and the *malagueña*.

[2] All flamenco singers sing someone else's songs. By the time a song gets to them it has passed through hundreds of singers and variations. Then the singer, consciously or not, adds his own variation—he adds himself.

Even when they deliberately try to imitate another's style, no matter how technically exact they are they never really do it. They have been anarchists too long. From childhood we are taught words and other social usages and we must use them in a particular way in order to get along in society, which is a structure made up of individuals who must relinquish most of their individuality in order to live within it. The artist is a person who knows and feels his own individuality more intensely than others, and so he is more reluctant to give it up. Someone else's sound is not adequate for his feeling. So he tries to create new patterns of words, brush strokes, or musical notes. He tries to make his own sound. Unlike the cultured artist, the flamenco singer neither "knows" nor "tries" to rebel. He simply does it every time he sings. He is an anarchist at birth, and being *andaluz* he is an anarchist linked to humanity through some age-long values. Every time one of my flamenco trio sings, he establishes his own difference. This moved me because I knew that most men were unable to make their own sound —that I had not yet made mine. I was struggling to enter the kingdom of *my* sounds and I was inspired by these men who were already liberated. Their very beings comforted me. And in the solitude of my farmhouse in the hills, as I began my own song, I kept hearing their varied lament in the clean, fresh sierra air.

That first night I spent in the Peña was a wonderful sherry wine that opened my intellectual, psychic, and sensory palate to what turned out to be an endless meal with unexpected sauces, flavors, and textures. While we were waiting downstairs, before the session began, a smooth, dapper, handsome man in his late twenties entered and was immediately the center of attention. I was surprised. He contrasted so strongly with the other weather-beaten, workworn faces that I thought he was just a passer-by. He couldn't be a part of this group. Was I wrong. He was not only a part, but a very essential one, and again to my surprise, when the singing began, *they sang to him*. In this my first lesson in the relation between singer and witness, I soon found out why. He knew when they were going through the motions and when they were singing fully. And he listened with unswerving concentration, reacting truthfully without false praise or reserved stinginess. It was my

38

first contact with the *cabal*, the supreme *aficionado*. He was Pepe Luque, the lawyer.

We quickly formed a friendship. We were both articulate intellectuals, we were both excited with the world of *cante*, and he generously offered me his deep knowledge. Whenever possible, I stopped at his house before going to the Peña. It was in a corner of the little square opposite the Bishop's Palace and the Cathedral of Málaga. Here was Pepe, the scion of a respected, wealthy family, implanted in the richly somber law office surrounded by law books and portraits of venerable forefathers, but his mind pulsated with thoughts on the world of flamenco. He had a tremendous record collection acquired through an inheritance from his grandfather and from tracking down old records in "antique" shops. He played me records of the old-time greats—the primitive sounds of Manuel Torres' *siguiriya*, the cultivated notes of Antonio Chacón's melodic *malagueña*, the tribal echo and wizardry of Pastora Pavón's *bulerías*—all mingled with the sound of running water from the fountain outside in the square. I was hungry to tap his unusual knowledge and insight and he was ready to express it to someone like me. For ten years he had been absorbed with this music, had made notes, and had dreamed secretly of writing authoritative essays on the subject. He was timid about writing. I was one of the catalysts in the flowering of his articulation. I encouraged him by listening passionately and with real interest. He treated me with a courtesy I always imagined was like that of the fabled Andalusian kings of antiquity. Without pomp there was something of the grand *señor* about him. He put his entire record collection at my disposal. He gave me so much of his time he had to sneak away from his law office across the hall and dodge prospective clients. Often he actually closed up the office to go off to make a recording or to play records and talk about flamenco.

But in spite of all this, strangely enough, it was difficult to create an intimate friendship with him, a friendship of the heart. He almost always kept his heart under control, surrounding it with fences of reserve and stability; equilibrium was to be maintained at all cost. It's not that he was cold or hostile. On the contrary, he was charming and went out of his way to help you. Part of it was that he despised weakness in those he considered superior. In himself. He felt that the superior person should not cry for help. For me, this was to ignore too much of the human condition and I was trying to work with the whole crazy puzzle. But it didn't matter. We still sought each other out and gave what we could. I would never have made such rapid progress in grasping the complexities of flamenco without his generosity. And here and there I saw moments when he tried to break out of his reserve. This happened often when the wine and the emotion of an intimate session hit him and he tried to sing. His whole being knew that in order to sing flamenco all reservations must be cast aside, that it was a hunt in a virgin forest where no compass, no trailmarks were permitted. You either got lost or came up with a magnificent specimen.

One long-playing record presents the *aficionado* of today with the styles of three generations. The new type of intellectual *aficionado*, like Pepe Luque and myself, knows, more or less, the history, the major interpreters, and the transformations of the past eighty years. Before 1920, the *aficionado* would have had to attend a thousand sessions to know a part of what we know today. But we, for the most part, have to recreate imaginatively certain norms, essences, historical rhythms he was born into. He *knew* how to be at a session. We have to learn it. And our historical consciousness creates new problems, because the intimate session, always the major focus of the art, can be wrecked by the slightest rational intrusion that ignores its basic norms. And no matter how true an *aficionado* the intellectual is, no matter how many good intentions he has, he tends to make anti-flamenco movements. He tends to talk against the singing or the silence. He tries to pre-shape a situation. He tries to introduce new dimensions that are antagonistic to the true session. For example, he permits a recital of cultured "flamencified" poetry, a hothouse orchid compared to the almond blossom of the sung *copla*, to be sandwiched in between the singing.

Pepe Luque, being a *cabal*, has no problem about how to *be* at a session, but he is in the middle of another dilemma: he finds himself, as an intellectual, making an *institution* out of an art. And this, by nature, deforms its spontaneity of expression. The problem is that eighty years ago flamenco was a living historical phenomenon. New styles were constantly being created by male and female artists. But today, and for the past thirty years, no new forms have arisen except for horrible attempts to "flamencify" popular songs and ballads. The singer is limited to imitating models of the past. But here is the crazy complexity: the history of Spain is the history of a nation that has spent its energy in resisting change. So that within certain Andalusians who have resisted certain modern manners of being flamenco is still very much alive. They imitate sounds of a past that is still alive within them. You can be very much a part of your times and not passively accept all its innovations or extremisms. You can reject what you feel is fraudulent in it. The spirit and the reality of the flamenco sound still has meaning for certain Andalusians. (Think of Ángel's son.) But it is also true that with each passing moment the new values, which have their new sounds, are *cutting away* flamenco's terrain. And so this is Pepe Luque's role: he finds himself a knight errant of flamenco art fighting to maintain a balance between the pure spontaneity of the closed-door session and the crusading didactic aim of the intellectual who wants to preserve and foment this purity. On the one hand, he knows that the best atmosphere for flamenco is a private room with a *few* dedicated singers, a guitarist who knows how and who loves to accompany, and a *few* dedicated witnesses. And, on the other hand, his desire to cut off the heads of the enemies and corruptors of flamenco art forces him to create an institution that will have the power and radius in the social structure to combat these adulterators. He is split down the middle. He is passionately content to spend endless hours merely listening to singing. But he just as much wants to be a leading crusader in the war against the heretics. Outwardly he will not admit the impossibility of fusing both passions within one structure such as the Peña. Inwardly he is filled with doubt and concern. The lawyer in him tries to conciliate, to settle the case "out of court." The *aficionado* in him knows that there is no settlement. Flamenco without intimacy is not flamenco. But a crusade needs soldiers to win the battle. Pepe Luque has become a sergeant at arms actively enlisting soldiers. He wants to enlist the best but inevitably a few cynical soldiers of fortune slip in. The intimate session balloons into a social institution.

Pepe Luque is a *señorito* and the history of Andalusia is linked to the phenomenon of the *señorito*. The word means young master, the son of the *señor*, the owner of the farm, shop, or profession. The worker and the farmhand and their wives and daughters have to conform to the orders, desires, and caprices of the *señorito*. Under normal conditions, he does not know hunger, want, material suffering. He either inherits the father's property or business or strikes out in a profession of his own. He does not see the world from the tense, gray waiting room; he is inside the office. Whatever spiritual stagnation Andalusia has undergone within the general Iberian decline is directly connected to the spiritual stagnation of the *señorito*. He is near the top of the social hierarchy and his intercourse is mostly with those who work for him or those of his own class. Therefore, he does not strive for new or higher goals. He has generally been content to preserve the beliefs and goals of the society he was born into. The intellectual and artistic curiosity of the average *señorito* is less than a monkey's. But since the eighteenth century, when the Spanish people began to elaborate a rich folk art in the forms of the bullfight, the popular theater, song and dance, there have always been those unusual *señoritos*, inflamed by one or all of these arts, who have rebelled against the spiritual barrenness in their own stratum and who have become passionate enthusiasts (*aficionados*) and patrons of these arts. For two centuries these arts nourished the people, the artists, and the thinkers—Goya, Galdós, Albéniz, the Machado brothers, Falla. García Lorca. Pepe Luque is in the center of this rich tradition.

The *señorito* paid for private fiestas; he imitated the manner of being of the flamenco and the *torero*; he secretly or openly accepted the stigma of being described as *muy flamenco*. In Andalusia, to call certain attitudes, acts, and people "flamenco" designates a capacity for abandon, a discarding of the rules imposed on us by society, a throwing off of the shackles of *have to*, a free giving and receiving. But it also suggests an association with the underworld. Flamenco stems from the tavern, the natural habitat of its creators and interpreters. Prostitution and assorted indecent spectacles also took place in the tavern and in its latter-day counterpart, the *café cantante*. Flamenco artists were not drunkards, whores, and pimps, but the stigma of their environment has always remained.

Pepe Luque's involvement with flamenco is an act of rebellion, whether he is conscious of it or not. It doesn't matter that for the past ten years a renaissance has been in movement, provoked by intellectuals who are attempting to expose the evils of a thirty-year decadence and who are trying to foment an enthusiasm for the pure styles. It doesn't matter that a new dimension of respectability is added through the membership of writers, musicians, academicians, historians, and government officials. The old stigma still remains, not only for the underworld associations but for another reason not usually brought out into the light. Whether the motives of the *aficionado* are to preserve a cultural treasure, or simply to be immersed in an expression that fills him, or both, the bare fact is this: the *aficionado* comes home at four or five in the morning, he cuts into the time of his profession, he cultivates friendships with those who are on the fringe of organized society, he forsakes rational control for the free spending implicit in the flamenco way of life. Otherwise he is not an *aficionado*. And this is a direct threat to the bourgeois way of life. Pepe Luque has grown as a human being precisely in the measure that his life as a flamenco has eaten away at his life as a *señorito*.

The *señorito* remains a *señorito* all his life on the material level. And most remain *señoritos* in the psychic area as well. Which means they float, on passive waves of comfort, through a still sea of inherited customs and institutions that shrink the soul rather than expand it. What distinguishes Luque from the mass of *señoritos* is, among other things, his growth through immersion in the world of flamenco. This world has put meat on the skeleton of his natural courtesy and curiosity. He knows that no external title or social distinction really counts at the moment of singing or listening to singing. And the singers sing to him because they respect his knowledge and they know he will not lie in his response. They respect him because they know he is *really* listening. This trait, which is one of the inner stances of the *cabal*, makes walking with him through the streets of Málaga a poignant promenade. He knows everyone, from the chief magistrate to the gypsy bootblack, and he talks to them all. But he does not condescend. If *señorear* means to deal with inferiors, it also indicates the ancient right of the people to be heard by the ruler, and Luque is a *señor* involved

43

in constant open-air audience. If he stops to speak with someone he really stops. Being *andaluz*, it is the measure of the other person's humanity that holds him. This is why he's always late for appointments.

One day I was to meet Pepe in Málaga. He showed up an hour and a half late. What happened? He had come from a case in court. His client had been sold a blind burro by a gypsy dealer, had refused to pay the rest of the money, and had demanded the return of the down payment. The atmosphere was more stock fair than law court. The two parties wanted to kill each other, the gypsy's relatives, what looked like a gathering of all the Andalusian clans, were belligerent onlookers, the lawyers were pleading for settlement, and even the judge, infected by the harangue, jumped in and begged for peace. Finally, Luque's client, realizing that the legal costs would outweigh the worth of the animal, gave in. The drama subsided into sentiment, the two parties left arm-in-arm, their lawyers with them, for a friendly drink to crown the event. With the wine and the good feeling the gathering turned into *juerga*, a spontaneous fiesta, the gypsy turned out to be a decent singer, and Luque had all he could do to tear himself away and meet me.

Pepe Luque taught me a deeper meaning of courtesy. He is directly responsible for the shucking off of an adolescent vision of courtesy confused with etiquette that I had when I came to Spain. Courtesy now means a relaxing of my ego *in time*, a giving of myself to the other person. The other great teachers of this vision of courtesy were the Andalusian peasants. Because they too are the *señores* of their land and their house even if they are only sharecroppers. They too stop what they are doing and attend to you. They too have time to be interested in who you are. It seems like such a simple thing: to have time for someone else. But when you are born into a society that is running from cradle to grave and then are placed in another one where the normal rhythm is a donkey-pace, you learn it's not so simple.

Pepe Luque tries to sing but he can't make the flamenco sound. At certain moments it seems as if he's approaching it, but a control over himself prevents him from reaching the necessary point where he would risk everything. In order to do this he would have to make some violent revolution in his blood, destroy the human history of his class, and become an anarchist. In the history of flamenco, the sound, with a few exceptions, has always come from the working class. (This theme would be a beautiful picnic for creative sociologists. As far as I know no one has tackled it up to now.) The bourgeois struggle has always been the avoidance of risk, of entering unknown areas. The daily rhythm of the bourgeois is the undisturbed beat of the secure niche, of a landscape that is always familiar. But in the daily quest for bread, the worker often finds himself in new places, a new construction job, a new wheat field, a new mine with a new boss watching, and his life is one of physical risk. This grappling with the song with risk of failure is what marks the true *cantaor*. But there is something else in the flamenco sound besides risk. Although he is a sensitive human being, Luque does not know what social exile is. He does not know the thorns of social frustrations that men at the bottom rung undergo every day. And despite the fact that he is very much of his class, that he continues to maintain the status quo, these things bother him because he would give a lot to make the flamenco sound. The fact that he can partially sing all the styles makes him an unusual *aficionado* because he knows what the singer has to strive for in each song. The *aficionado* who cannot sing at all will always find a gap between himself and the singer. Which is my case. For three years I listened to a lot of flamenco and never opened my beak. But then I began humming and croaking all over the place. I'm on another planet as to the sound. It comes out more like Frank Sinatra than like flamenco but I don't care. I dream that one day a miracle will happen and I'll be able to do it.

Why am I writing about Pepe Luque? Because, apart from the fact that he ushered me into the world of flamenco, that through him I was focused immediately on the genuine and the pure, he is a living symbol of Andalusia today. He belongs to a diminishing minority that resists certain changes harmful to what is vital and positive—changes in social and human intercourse. Yet he is very much a part of his times. In him flow all the artistic traditions, both cultured and popular, as well as the social and religious ones. A personal grace, an esthetic sensibility, a deep sense of courtesy, a solid stance of personal dignity, an appetite for *gracia*—all these enable him to move easily in any world. Like Diego, Manolillo, and Ángel, he is a certain prototype of *andaluz*, and therefore, as Juan Ramón Jiménez says, universal. In spite of continuing the social and religious conventions that, I feel, imprison a unique spirit, he is a good example of that Spanish apolitical democratic attitude that leaps over all social barriers and responds to personal qualities. And if I write about the armor around his heart and a behavior of conciliation that prevents him from wielding his potential, it's all right; he is still young and is only beginning to grow. It is among the Pepe Luques that Spain must look to salvage its vital authenticity in the coming decades of change. It's not enough to resist such changes as the creation of a Miami Beach in Spain by opposing them with a select traditional expression such as flamenco. This gives identity to a Pepe Luque but it will not satisfy the coming generations. They will need new social norms to replace those that have already withered. If I preach revolution to Pepe in the form of a relentless struggle for self-truth and the vulnerability of an open heart, he has shown me that one can give *within* convention and tradition. He has enlarged my vision of his people's history through the living history of his own person. Whether he knows it or not, he is in the center of historic change. He wants to retain certain traditions while letting in worlds that will change those same traditions. He wants to proselytize in the world yet live in a cloister at the same time. He wants to be a *señorito* and a flamenco, a patriot and an internationalist. He wants to preserve the sanctity of the intimate session yet expand the Peña Juan Breva. Whatever happens in the struggle Luque will no longer be the conservative young *señorito* I first knew. He will by force become a man.

5

Yo no soy de esta tierra
ni conozco a nadie
aquel que haga un bien conmigo
que Dios se lo pague.

I'm not from this land
I know no one here
Whoever is good to me
May God reward him.

I started going into Málaga three or four times a week. I sat in the public archives and read everything there was on flamenco. The first exciting discovery was the work of Anselmo González Climent, a young Argentine, spearhead of the new literary interest in flamenco. His books were a rich, dynamic statement of what I was intuiting and observing in the sessions at the Peña. González Climent sits in the very center of the flamenco universe, coupling a creative erudition with a deep insight into the essences of the flamenco drama. Reading him was to sit in some fantastic session where I was simultaneously singer and witness.

The past and the present, the styles and the singers, the gestures and the exegeses—all merged in the pages of his books, which were a happy spiritual complement to the intensity of live flamenco phenomena. Without the experience of his books my assimilation of flamenco events would have been greatly retarded. The vast difference between González Climent and the majority of other writers on flamenco is that he always works from a vision of the whole. He writes:

> The true flamenco dimension of an expression is the result of its particular plastic forms, of the chance temperament of the interpreter who gives it life, and finally, of the receptive richness of the listener. If this triad of conditions is fully offered, any song can enclose the most attractive virtues of the workings of flamenco. The singers generally know how to adapt themselves to the previous attitude each style demands, to such a degree that perception and choice attain considerable refinement. The singer takes into account—apart from his unique perilous personal moment—the fluctuating quality of profundity that his public may have, the capacity of refinement of the *cabales*, the vital insinuation of the hour, the general march of the night, the place, the wines. . . . This coordination is realized with rapidity and amazing exactitude. None of these details is useless or discarded. To be careless of this order of things is to break the subtle and coincidental miracle of the flamenco session.[1]

This translation only suggests the language that González Climent has forged to fit the flamenco event. His work is an ideal guitar accompanying the song of the flamenco experience: he never loses himself in precious filigrees but his rich, artistic personality always comes through.

I sat in the archives and studied. The archivist, Francisco Bejarano, was a member of the Peña. His was one of the little flames of simple cordiality that warmed me in my pilgrimage through the boulevards and backstreets of flamenco. Though he is a correct, efficient government employee, carefully separating his official life from his personal activities, the very fact that he is an *aficionado* brings him into magical regions closed to his colleagues. That he

---

[1] Translated by the author from *Bulerías: Un ensayo jerezano* (Jerez de la Frontera: Cátedra de Flamencología, 1961), pp. 16–17.

needs to listen from time to time to this particular music that is traditional yet passionately personal sharply distinguishes him from the dry academician. Ten years before the mainstream of literary production, Don Francisco was publishing articles on flamenco in the Málaga press. They were just the way he is: modest, informative, richly historical, with a stroke of creativity in the summing-up. There is something angelic about Don Francisco. A bushy-browed, dreamy, yet shrewd angel who does not want to lead men; he prefers to help them. It's as if the classical spirit of being a keeper of archives has entered his person and it doesn't matter whether strangers ask him for old manuscripts or for tobacco; he attends everyone with the same precise, kind care and, if it is provoked, with the same impish humor.

I sat in the archives, read all his articles, and asked questions. The fact that Don Francisco, Manolillo, Pepe Luque belonged to the Peña began to overwhelm me. They are of such different cultural backgrounds, vocations, classes, temperaments, generations —yet all are involved with *cante* and all participate without losing their individuality. This amazed me. All the social groups I had ever known had always demanded the sacrifice of the individual in return for a common vision, a common action. The Peña works in reverse. The group was always subjected to the individual spark or caprice. Sometimes the individualism resulted in vulgarity and chaos, but it was endured and eventually equilibrium was restored. I learned about endurance. In all human intercourse there are bad-tasting moments. The choice is to walk out or to wait. How many times, in the beginning, I left a session out of impatience and the next day learned that it had taken a turn into a beautiful moment! But I was a New Yorker and the New Yorker is not taught to wait. If the grilled-cheese sandwich comes sixty seconds late he is already fidgeting on his stool. The *andaluz* has lived within a rhythm of waiting for a few thousand years. Some call it vegetating, others, enduring. But at any rate, the anarchy of the Peña—sometimes sweet, sometimes comic, absurd, irritating, ennobling—was a balm annointing all the lacerations caused by my perpetual butting against the prevailing social values. I had finally found a place where I could be a rebel to my heart's content within a traditional order that I had to fathom at the same time. I had finally found a society where integrity was a working essence. For me, who had never been able to function in a group, this was terribly important. It helped smash the tight, hard shell I had grown in order to face the world.

Eighty years ago, *aficionados* would enter one of the private rooms the taverns had in those days—and still have wherever the mechanical hand of progress has not swept them away—would sit and talk and drink a while, and then someone would begin to sing. The singer might be professional or amateur, but the result always depended on the changing alchemy of three basic components: what styles were sung, the quality of the singer, and the knowing receptivity of the listeners. If the *aficionados* were authentic, no one was admitted who was not an intelligent lover of *cante*, and the number was always kept small to preserve intimacy. Thus the ideal *juerga* got its name: "the closed-door session." In those days there were many great singers who never stepped onto a stage. There was no radio, no cinema, no phonograph. *Cante* was a major expression and emotional outlet for the *andaluz*. The *juerga* was an everyday occurrence and both professionals and amateurs kept its dynamics alive. And though it was an art form derived from and sustained by the lower classes, it was not mass entertainment. The subtleties, the discretion, the deep integrity, the extensive sensibility involved have always kept *cante* in the hands of a select minority. What happened was that, in its evolution, from about 1920 on, certain saccharine adulterations were introduced and flamenco penetrated the popular theatre as another form of musical entertainment. From this moment there were essentially two kinds of singer: the ones who performed in the theatre, joining the ranks of what was called the incredible name of *opera flamenca*,[2] and the ones who continued to sing in the diminishing closed-door sessions, either for money or as amateurs. The first embarked on a modernization and a corruption and the latter kept alive the classical forms. The one made money, the other eked out a sporadic living or worked at a trade. As Spain caught up with

[2] The *opera flamenca* was an operetta with pseudo-flamenco components of dance, guitar, and a virtuoso warbler. This thin potpourri was the father of the current flamenco "show."

the twentieth century, the *andaluz* turned to other forms of artistic expression. But the closed-door session survived.

Moments of true flamenco can occur in an infinite number of settings but there is no atmosphere superior to the closed-door session. Its elements are ritualistic intimacy, spontaneity, intelligent passion, integrity, and no coercion from without. It is difficult for any other flamenco setting to contain even one of them. Perhaps the closest is the spontaneous drunken singing in a bar, but almost always some intruder breaks the thread. When I first entered the Peña Juan Breva it was something like a twentieth-century grandchild of the closed-door session. But eighty years of history had passed and thirty of flamenco decadence. From the very beginning there was a split in the men of the Peña. On the one hand there were those who came to sing and to listen, more or less aware of what terms like "classical," "impurities," "corruptions" meant, but reacting to these terms through the actual singing, and on the other hand there were those intellectuals who wanted to combine the rhythms of the closed-door session with a didactic, active crusade against the adulterators. In the beginning this worked beautifully since the members were few. Gradually the informal gatherings crystalized into regular, Saturday night meetings, and Pepe Luque drew up a charter:

Fundamental Norms
Proclamation of Principles

Gathered in Málaga, by the grace of God, we, the components of the Peña Juan Breva, proclaim as basis and goal of our institution and decisive guide of our common conduct the following regulations, to which we promise eternal faithfulness:

First point: To study or investigate with scientific ambition the extensive subject that, with more or less propriety, is understood by the term *cante flamenco*.

Second point: To guard *cante* in all its purity and integrity, denouncing the bad, and fighting against all adulterators and against unfortunate innovators or creators, whatever their relation to flamenco art may be.

Third point: To foment enthusiasm for *cante*, making it better-known, since from knowledge is born appreciation.

These three points, in synthetic expression, form the motto

51

of the Peña Juan Breva, triple postulate, which, always referring to *cante*, is prayed like this:

> To Continue Learning
> To Keep Vigil Over Purity
> To Disseminate By Teaching.

Málaga, November 22, 1958[3]

I came to the Peña in the spring of 1960. Diego had described it as "a place where I and some friends go to sing." The world was made up, for him, of places where you could sing and places where you couldn't. This meant that in those days there was still an equilibrium between the singing and the scientific aims. There still existed some marvelous unanimity of feeling that knew when words were excess and when the sounds of *cante* were needed. No president had to direct movements. Diego or Manolillo tuned up with a preparatory *ay* and there was immediate silence. The singing lasted until midnight when Emilio, the owner of the Casa Luna, came up to announce closing time. The outside world was invading the free spending implicit in the flamenco way of being, and so the last moments were an intense *summum* of the deepest songs that each man carried within. The singing continued on the staircase, in the antechamber downstairs, in the streets. And if a bar could be found open it lasted until the early morning hours. This was the Peña I first knew. But it lasted this way only about a year and a half.

Then the Peña started to expand. It organized several national contests and a growing aura of popularity invaded its obscure existence. It broadcast on the radio and took part in a theatrical show; the government and high society became aware of it, and now touristic projects are being planned around it. A new charter, with directing officials and a long list of regulations, was drawn up and there are now about two hundred fifty members. One of the reasons for the expansion was to get enough paying members to be able to rent a larger, independent meeting place, a reasonable need. But in the meantime, too many men, bad or indifferent *aficionados*, became members. They were interested in extra-flamenco activities:

---

[3] Translation by the author.

in placing the Peña into other cultural institutions and in forming a social and recreational club. The Peña broadened its scope but lost, to a great extent its most precious quality: its pure flamenco atmosphere. It lost the human intimacy of a few friends exchanging feelings, ideas, laughter, and subtle artistic expression. It exchanged a unique manner of being for one of varied, conflicting interests. It exchanged artistic and human unity for petty and profound disunity. But the saddest change of all is that *the singer no longer feels at ease there.* Too much extraneous verbal noise shatters the flamenco silence needed for introspection. Perhaps in the new locale, on off evenings, it will be regained. But as of now the Peña has broken ties with the heritage of the closed-door session. Nonflamenco worlds have replaced the world of flamenco.

What was my role in the Peña? I came in, a foreigner, ignorant of flamenco, but I was *simpático,* had a certain gift of gab, and although one never totally learns a foreign language I spoke Spanish well enough to get through to them. I was a novelty, but they sensed my desire to learn and my movements seemed right to them. They couldn't quite place me, though. I had *cultura,* as they put it, meaning I was literate and educated, but I didn't view the world from a stance of defending any vested interests, any particular class or religion. Since I'd had a history of working with my hands, I wasn't quite a *señorito,* but neither was I a proletarian. They couldn't categorize me but it didn't matter. My oddness was explained by the fact that I was a foreigner, and since in the beginning I sat quietly and listened with visible enjoyment they took me into the fold. They didn't suspect that through intense desire I would accumulate knowledge in one year that the average *aficionado* takes ten to learn. And what excited me was that the more I learned the more I saw how much more there was to learn. They didn't and still don't know that something important was happening to me because of my contact with them. That my whole past and present flowed into the sessions and that I was flowering because of the rich soil. That every time I left them I was terribly excited by the many big and little happenings, excited by my own excitement, aware that my battered, breathing self had finally found—after all those years of exile—a *society,* but one of *indi-*

viduals. And why did they meet? To sing to each other. Outside, in that other world, men were jockeying and maneuvering and conneuvering to get the jump on killing each other, and here they were, singing. I had finally found a group within which I could express my artistic and moral self, which was in the process of being beautifully replenished. Little wonder that I was dying to know why and what this music was that had brought me and these men together.

To be a foreigner in Spain is to be a unique phenomenon. Even after so many years, every time I go to town I walk the gauntlet of tireless, unabashed, open-mouthed stares. You get the feeling there is something freakish about you, as if you had actually grown extra appendages. Moreover, after a while, you start seeing the other recently arrived foreigners as freaks because you are already viewing them from within a different time sense and gesture sense. If you are really interested in this new world around you, if you admire it, you pick up new ways of being and doing. Then when you see an English couple in an Andalusian market, he attired in a pair of ballooning Bermuda shorts that expose flesh the color of a tortured lobster and she in shorts and bobby socks, they seem ludicrous to you. Beyond the attire and the appearance, it's because they are shopping *as if they were either in some genteel English grocer's or in the heart of the African jungle.* They are totally unaware of their surroundings. But curiously enough, as much as the Spaniard is finely attuned to differences, he is to the same degree psychically deaf to *similarities.* He is firmly convinced that the foreigner can never really understand him or his ways. This stems, partially, from a natural vanity that has been strengthened by centuries of isolation. The men of the Peña see me more or less like this: "Pablo has a real feeling for flamenco and it's remarkable how much he loves it. Of course, being a foreigner, he can't really know it like a Spaniard but it doesn't matter: *we enjoy seeing him enjoy himself.*"

One night several years ago, after a Saturday session, a few of us went to Alfonso's, a little restaurant-bar on Calle Granada. Alfonso is an artist who makes a fantastic consommé which, combined with sips of Montilla wine, mellows the by-this-time mellow body to a rosy, responsive, fraternal temper. We stood there drinking, and one of the men came over to me and said affectionately: "Pablo, please don't be offended but there's something I've been meaning to ask you for a long time. *Do you really know flamenco?* No, I'm serious, I know you've been listening for a few years and you're really interested in it, I know you're writing about it, but tell me—do you *really* understand it? Tonight I was watching you and when Ángel sang what I thought was good and I felt like saying *ole,* I heard you say *ole.* When so-and-so sang what I thought was bad, I saw you lower your head and keep silent. Listen, I'm Spanish, and I'm not always sure of the styles and the quality but you, do you really *know* it?" He said this so sweetly into my already grinning face I couldn't help but embrace him and I stammered out some modest reply. I didn't tell him about my three years of passionate involvement that were equivalent to I don't know how many ordinary years. I didn't tell him that González Climent had written it all out, had shown me the right paths to follow the same way Diego, Manolillo, Ángel, and Pepe Luque had. He didn't know about all the hours I'd spent talking with them, listening to them sing, listening to records in Luque's house. He had never seen me in the archives with Don Francisco. He just saw me occasionally in the Peña and was shaken to the marrow of his Spanish psychology. How could a foreigner know or seem to know about flamenco?

This same attitude in a person whose vanity is tinged by hypocrisy and cowardice can be very ugly. One night, in a discussion which wasn't turning out too well for him, an acquaintance of one of the members, a man who had just spent eight years in Argentina, let loose with: "You the foreigner look on us as if we were rare insects. You can never understand us. We hate differently, we love differently, we worship differently, we sing differently. You can never understand this. We are *machos,* virile males, and you the Anglo-Saxon do not know what this is." I was an American, therefore Anglo-Saxon. He didn't know that my grandmother was born in Poland and my grandfather in Austria. That my parents were raised in New York's East Side ghetto. But he doesn't see an individual face before him. He doesn't hear particular speech. He hears and he sees what he understands by "American," "German," "Frenchman," etc. And he speaks about "we Spaniards."

His is a mentality that breeds a destructive provincialism, a vanity of the isolated and isolating ego—evils that have prolonged Spain's history of being closed to the few positive currents these past two centuries. Next to him is sitting Cayetano, big, somber, friendly Cayetano, who only opens his mouth when he has something to say. Who knows nothing about half-tones, or what the musical definition of *falsetto* is, or who is responsible for the decadence of flamenco. But Cayetano knows how to ask for songs and how to listen: subtle psychological and esthetic perceptions that distinguish the true *aficionado* from the empty theoretician.

So I learned the ideal gestures, inner and outer (yes one can learn gestures and live with them until they become part of one's breathing self); I leaned towards and learned the ritualistic elements in the closed-door session. I was shown the false, adulterated ways of singing, the false ways of listening—and I became a Frankenstein. Elated by an art form that demanded integrity from its performer and its witness, I refused to compromise with the impurities that cropped up. I witnessed the change from meetings where a few united individuals spent hours of communal delight to those that were sprawling, chaotic, bitter with envy, dominated by banal talk, and I protested. I got up at one of the sessions, knees trembling, and voiced a year of disgust and apprehension. I tried to tell them it was a change from within that was needed and my tirade struck with the force of a marshmallow. Each one turned the words to suit his own perceptions and opinions. I called for a return to the dignity and the ritual of the closed-door session and they thought a bell to sound order would solve the problem. It was a powerful lesson. I realized that the Peña was now a group, like any other group, and that revolutionary change within each individual could not be achieved simply by asking for it.

I still go to the Peña, not as often, but I still get excited and dream that maybe this time it'll be like it was. That maybe some miracle will occur and only a few of the original members and singers will show up and it'll be like before. And of course, no matter what happens to the Peña, it's enough for me to spend a few hours with those few unique individuals who are beyond any institutional changes around them. One of Spain's problems is that when this kind of person miraculously appears, the other Spaniards do their best to crush his body and imprison his spirit.

I want to talk about the human essences of two men, essences so strong they imbue others with them and carry everyone for hours into a magical garden of sounds, sensations, emotions. I think of Pepe Navarro and the first time I met him. It was in Luque's house; we had been listening to records, and in came a tall, brown, nervous, talkative man of about fifty, with a smile hovering between a caress and a tease, who literally collared me when he learned I was an *aficionado*. When I told him I didn't know the *malagueña*, he sang five or six different styles in delicate high-pitched strokes, his vocal chords gone. I think of all the miserable, pussyfooting, suspicious beginnings with people, yet this man was singing to me thirty seconds after we said "hello." I had to catch a train, but he held me and sang still another song, then put me on the back of his motorcycle, and we raced across Málaga to the station.

Pepe Navarro's father had owned a theatre in Álora through which all the old-time great singers passed. As a young boy he used to sneak in late at night to listen and hang around the dressing rooms. Pepe Navarro is one of the most passionate *aficionados* I've ever met. He's lived forty years with *cante* and can sing all the styles. He has notebooks with explanations of each style which he generously offered me. But it is as a practicing *aficionado* in the center of the intimate session where all his passion and articulation illumine most—in that moment when the wine has made singer and witness responsive and the three or four good singers of the Peña infect each other and carry a certain style into a symphony of individual variations. Pepe Navarro is essential for the divine *juerga*, when the session hovers between lament and merriment, dipping its wings in both. Then he becomes both well and source, laughter and sorrow, comrade and isolated entity, and he ceaselessly gives and gives. Intensely involved in explanation, in history, in didactic argument, he is equally capable of spending four hours in an obscure bar or on a street corner *just singing and listening*. Material problems have absented him from the Peña for a number of years. It suffers from the loss of his dynamic, sensitive presence.

Antonio Villodre: chunky, pugnosed, that massive bull's head always thrusting the direct glance, the direct smile, and the deep hoarse voice in full greeting. Antonio Villodre is one of those *aficionados* who, although he can enjoy the whole gamut of *cante*, leans personally in his own singing and in his deeper emotions to the *jondo* styles: *siguiriyas, soleares, deblas, martinetes*. I learned so much just by watching him *listen*, watching him shake off requests to sing, watching him wait until *his* moment surged from within and then I listened to the voice hovering between aphonia and rich huskiness:

> *Estoy derramando más lágrimas*
> *que agua lleva un río*
> *por unos ojitos negros y rajados*
> *que se me han perdido.*

> I'm shedding more tears
> Than the river has water
> Because of almond black eyes
> That are my ruin.

I watched him sitting there quietly, rolling a cigarette, once in a while entering the heated discussions, but mostly remaining aloof. He had the gravity, sometimes heavy, sometimes precise, of old countrymen you see sitting in the cafés: he emanated the same aura of solemnity. Except that suddenly it was broken by a sound that wounded the air with metallic sobbing and a struggling, extended line of anguish. In the person of Antonio Villodre, who is in his early fifties, I saw clearly, as with Manolillo, the social, human, and generational differences that separate one Spaniard from another today. He is much closer to Manolo than to Ángel. Though a railroad worker, he is closer to rural rhythms than to urban ones. He is a continent away from the average *señorito* of thirty and a planet away from the young *niño bonito* of twenty who is dancing the twist. It's in his face and in the way he greets you. In his anecdotes about the past and about his father. In the way he behaves in the closed-door session. It's in the way he rolls his cigarette. He too, as a boy in short pants, risking a beating from his father, sneaked in to hear Manuel Torres in a theatre one night. Like Pepe Navarro, he has lived with flamenco rhythms since childhood.

So on the one hand I read in González Climent's books how the true *aficionado* acted, and on the other, I saw it operating in Antonio Villodre and in Pepe Navarro. Is it any wonder I learned quickly?

An ideal session. An ideal session that happened. I get off the train, joke with the waiter at the station bar. He is a huge picaresque eye writing his own novels on the people that drift into his radius. He has already told me which woman he prefers among those he has seen with me. On into Málaga. Check in at the *pensión*. The charwoman is twinkling as soon as she sees me; her eyes say, "You old rascal"; her voice says, "Single or double?" I answer, "Don't know yet." She laughs and pokes the other maid in the ribs. A tapestry of salutations with the family that owns the *pensión*. Don Carlos, Don Eduardo, Margarita. Each his little joke, his little greeting. On the staircase Eduardo hums his *fandanguillo*, knowing I'm listening. Don Pablo is in Málaga. That means somewhere there'll be singing. I wash up and go out into the street. Around the corner to Bar Guerola. There's Valeriano in grey-haired fatigue, tossing me a deep bemused smile. Valeriano has the face of a ruined Mephistopheles and is the most vital pessimist I have ever known: his words bite into the hypocrisy and injustice of Spain. I sip a glass of red Valdepeñas and plunge into the sulphur and almond blossom of his eyes that say, "I'm suffering, I know why I'm suffering, I'm a comrade when *I* feel like it." Out into the street. Elaborate greeting and handshake with the tobacco seller who says, "I'm glad to see you," and proceeds to tell me his latest trials and tribulations. This is why I love Málaga: every little movement is personal. You're never a lost cipher as in the metropolis. Cigars in my pocket for Manolillo and Ángel and I'm headed for "Casa Matías" to get a hot, juicy plate of veal stew, to sop up the sauce with extra bread and wash it down with a big glass of wine. Cigar lit, I saunter up Calle Nueva, eyeing the voluptuous *malagueñas* out for the Saturday evening *paseo* and I cross the Plaza de la Constitución. Here the shape of the next hour depends on what flamencos I run into. There are the pros in front of the "Central."

Those who are working in the Torremolinos clubs are all togged out, hair gleaming. If no one is around, I check the usual bodegas and bars, sampling the wines and beers: "La Buena Sombra," "El Pombo," "La Campana," Augustin's kiosk in the Plaza de la Merced, Alfonso's. If I'm feeling quiet I call Luque and maybe go to his house to chat and hear some records. But there's Manolillo, strutting like the mayor of Málaga, with a grin that could sustain you all day. We embrace and go for a drink. Maybe we run into Diego, dapper and alone, tuning up for the evening's singing or else anchored on the deep sea floor of some memory and then there's the usual teasing banter between him and Manolo. If I'm lucky Diego lets me draw him out and he sings, standing there in the bar, low-voiced and intimate:

> *El gallo en su gallinera*
> *se sacude y luego canta*
> *el que duerme en cama ajena*
> *de madrugada le levantan.*

> The cock in his henhouse
> Shakes himself then sings
> He who sleeps in another's bed
> Has to get up at dawn.

> *Te miro de arriba abajo*
> *pero te veo tan niña*
> *y el querer me cuesta trabajo.*

> I look you up and down
> I see you're too young
> And it's hard to love you.

And then, the three of us, our faces different hues of wine red, our spirits in an intimate plaza of exuberance, stroll up Calle Granada toward Casa Luna and the Peña.

The bar is packed with the usual Saturday night patrons. There's Santoro, his deep voice booming out a greeting. Emilio is having his hands full serving everyone. He hands us a bottle of wine and glasses and we start upstairs. There's Pepe Luque, Don Francisco, Don Ricardo, Pepe Flújar, Antonio Villodre, Cuevas, Rafael, Cayetano. They're sitting having the first quiet drink. The greetings, the handshakes, the teasing smoke the air for a few minutes. Manolillo sits down and pours wine for everyone. Pepe Luque puts on the national anthem: the *fandango* of Juan Breva. For the thousandth time there is praise for the wild, sonorous magic of this singer who died forty-five years ago but who is reborn every Saturday night in this little room. The "tinned" music shifts from Juan Breva's rustic lilt to the tribal accents of Pastora Pavón. We accompany her with *oles*, head-shaking smiles, and wreaths of silent praise. Through the door come Ángel and Pepe Navarro with more wine and spiced comments. Pepe Navarro throws his arms around me and asks where I've been hiding. Ángel says: "Kennedy, how are you?" The atmosphere quiets down. We listen to Tomás Pavón and his long impossible-lunged chant *por soleares*. Then no one says anything but we all know it: the period of "tinned" music is over. There is silence or a low murmur. Diego, eyes half-closed, tunes up *por malagueñas*. He leans forward in his chair and carries us, through the aged temple of his voice, to some abandoned ruin where the wind bends the necks of wild weeds and blows through the broken walls:

> *Desde que te conocí*
> *mi corazón llora sangre*
> *yo me quisiera morir*
> *porque mi pena es muy grande*
> *y así no puedo vivir.*

> Since I've known you
> My heart weeps blood
> I want to die
> For my sorrow is so deep
> And I can't live this way.

Diego sings again, ends with his boyish smile, half-timid, half-triumphant, and reaches for his wine. Ángel tunes up *por soleares*, accompanies himself with his wizard handclap and sings five or six songs mounting in emotion and strain. Something has happened to the singers and the witnesses tonight. The *cante por soleares* has crept in past the outer skin of sensation and linked everyone to its search for equilibrium within passion. Diego enters the search with the *soleares* of Rafael Moreno, drowning himself in the difficult extensions. Pepe Navarro follows in that fluted whisper of a whisper and now Villodre stirs himself to sing in the style of Manuel Torres. Time is a flamenco cantata *por soleares*. A mountain spring flowing down to the sea through four arroyos. We pause at the seashore to catch our breath, drink wine, hurl words into the waves. Members come and go. In comes Santoro. Santoro sang the first night I came to the Peña. He drinks downstairs with friends and then appears at a late hour and tries to sing *por siguiriyas*. Since that first night he has never been able to finish the song. Why? Because to complete a *siguiriya* legitimately is a gift given to a few privileged beings. Santoro is the flesh and soul of every *aficionado* dying to sing but unable to do it. I swear the day I can sing one song *completely*, even if only half-decently, I'll take him off to some quiet corner and sing to him. And we'll both get fat from the joy of it.

The singing continues. Manolillo breaks the lull with the songs of "El Piyayo," the picaresque verse and his inimitable *gracia* spread smiles throughout the room. Diego, who has been silent for some time, is untouched by this lighter mood. He sits in a private room of his own sounds and emerges only when he sings. He takes us from the sunny wink and tease of "El Piyayo" to the dark grotto of the *cante por siguiriyas*. But in his melodious non-*siguiriya* voice I see the sun through the chinks in the rock. It is a delicate dirge with a few tones of anguish. But this movement into the terrain of the *siguiriya* has stirred Villodre and he sings it in the classical manner: where despair shatters melody and the *ay* and the sob take over. From the defiant anguish of the *siguiriya* to the half-defiant, half-helpless weeping of the *martinete* are but a few silent steps. And Manolo, the smith, wields the hammer: terse, plaintive strokes that end, in the last line's extending strain, with the real or metaphorical upraised fist. Ángel and Villodre continue with their versions of the *martinete*. We sit at the edge of a well, each one looking in and hearing his own nuance of the same echo, and Emilio comes in announcing closing time. No one moves. Emilio goes downstairs. The singing continues. Villodre, in great form tonight, sings the *caña*. Ángel can't keep it in any longer. Something is eating him up tonight and he must give it form through the weeping tones of the *fandanguillo* of "El Car-

bonero." Pepe Navarro, high as a kite, trails Ángel with the
malagueña of "Chacón." A violent discussion breaks out over some
intricate drop or rise in the song. Don Francisco asks for silence,
mock-threatening to sing. And he asks Diego to sing *por soleares*
again. Half an hour has passed. Emilio comes up again and with a
completely transparent act of grimness, orders us to leave. We tell
him okay. He leaves. No one moves. Pepe Flújar, so mellow by this
time, gets up enough courage to sing the *petenera*. This permits
the lesser singers to express their feelings through song. Emilio
comes in again. We all get up, the cost of the wine is divided among
the members, and standing there, Villodre breaks out into a *debla*.
Manolo and Ángel cap it with *martinetes*. We start to leave in
dispersed clumps. Six steps are taken to the staircase. Pepe Navarro, remembering that hours ago I told him I didn't know the
malagueña of "El Perote," collars me and begins singing again.
Everyone stops to listen. Ángel follows up with the *malagueña* of
Enrique, "El Mellizo." Diego sings *por La Trini*. We finally make
it downstairs to the little antechamber behind the bar. The doors
are closed. Only a few of the regular patrons of the Casa Luna
remain. A big discussion is in full blast at the bar—whether they
sang better in the old days or now. In the antechamber, near the
urinal, Manolillo is singing "El Piyayo" again. Ángel keeps it alive
with *alegrías*. There's a divine chaos. Little groups arguing and
singing. Finally, it's time to go. Emilio really has to close up. We
say good night and there in the street, I swear I'm not exaggerating,
the talking and the singing continue. Sure, more dispersed and in
half-voice, but the sense of time and space is completely drenched
in the aromatic spirits of flamenco. The Peña breaks up into little
groups who say they are going home. I'm with Ángel, Manolo, and
Diego, and we're walking Pepe Luque home. With us are Don
Ricardo and Don Francisco. Don Francisco, smiling and humming
to himself *por soleares*, says: "Maybe 'Bar Maese' is still open and
we can have a last one." Manolo: "Never say 'the last one.' The
next to the last one." Luque: "It's late; I really have to go home."
I say: "One quick one, Pepe, that's all." Luque: "Okay, if it's a
quick one, okay." "Bar Maese" is still open. There are two groups
of men drinking. One, aged between fifty and sixty, and the other,
between twenty and thirty. Manolillo and Ángel know everyone

(is there a bar in Málaga where they don't know someone?) and a round of Montilla is ordered. Among the young group someone is singing *fandanguillos*. Pretty, high-voiced, pleasant, but so thin compared to what we've been hearing all night. Ángel, Manolillo, and Diego carry another half-hour of singing between them. All these time calculations are very approximate. I'm so high now. And tired. How do they do it: sing and drink and laugh and joke all night long? Everyone in the bar, young, middle-aged, old, is held by the singing. It's one of those rare nights when no drunk and no imbecile breaks the mood. I'm standing in a bar in Málaga. The Costa del Sol. Outside, and all up and down the coast, the plague fevers of greed are raging. The sad, ludicrous, circus rhythms of resort pleasures in picturesque, sunny Andalusia are in full swing. Ugly fishing villages are being converted into Miami Beach and Saint Tropez. Huge hotels, jail-like, except for the pastel facades, are being erected against landscapes of olive groves. Progress and prosperity have come to Spain. And never before in its history, save for that other war, the Civil War, have so many verbal agreements been broken in so short a time.

But here in a bar, a foreigner and three generations of Andalusians are linked, for one brief miraculous moment, by three men singing. The bar closes up and we walk Luque home. Ángel goes up to an all-night inn in the hills of Málaga to continue singing. Manolo walks me to my *pensión* where I swim in the bed for a while and finally fall asleep. And Manolo. Next morning at the train station he is waiting for me, freshly shaven and so alive. He says: "Come on, I'll buy you a shot to straighten you out. What a night! On the way home I ran into some friends . . . and I got in at five. You coming in next week? Okay, I'll meet you in front of the 'Central' at seven." I get on the train and return to Fuengirola.

An ideal session. A session that happened.

6

Fui piedra y perdí mi centro
y m'arrojaron ar má
y ar cabo de mucho tiempo
mi centro volví a encontrá.

I was a stone, I lost my center
And they threw me into the sea
And after a long time
I found my center again.

*I*n May, 1961, I left Málaga in search of other
horizons. I was a bee hunting more and more nectar; I wanted to
hear other singers and I wanted to find out what flamenco meant
to other Andalusians. I wondered if I could walk into a strange
environment and be recognized as an *aficionado*. Everyone had told
me that in Cádiz and Seville there were more and better singers,
that flamenco was more alive there, and I went to see if it was true.
I had very little money: I hitchhiked and took buses. And, as I

wandered around in the guise of a "journalist from the North,"[1] hoping they would never ask me what North, a strange and beautiful thing happened that I mull over now. Four years before in 1957, my first trip to Spain, I had wandered through the same towns, alone and lonely, so desperate to embrace a woman, to run into a man who would see my passion for his country and who would bring me into the life of the town. But it never happened. I was stewing in my own loneliness, playing the role of the exiled poet, and this brooding choked off a natural curiosity, strangled the unfolding of circumstance that was being born *then*, right there in that next moment. I froze my true feelings into an aloof, superior, don't-touch-me expression and I'm sure I chilled more than one passerby with this idiotic mask. I was going to be strong and stoical and not show my emotions. Now I see how absurd this was. Hundreds of situations might have blossomed had I left myself open to them. But there was something else in the way. For ten years, in America, I had forged an image of Spain based on literature, and I floated through this image *condescending* to the reality around me. I snobbishly and stubbornly haunted places and quarters that fit my prefabricated image and refused to admit any other. But that image was a Spain that had ended in 1936 and it was 1957. I sat in the bars mingling with the people, the abstract people, but I almost never entered the life of one individual. And so, clinging to my condescension and to my pre-vision, I killed off the essence of real travel which is to transplant the roots of our being into a soil of new circumstance, new realities. I sat in the cafés, scribbling in my notebook, but I never thought to write about what was happening to me. I scribbled pretty surface impressions but what I was really thinking was: "Somebody, anybody, please ask me to go home with you."

But now it was different. I was alone but not lonely. Now I entered a town and asked: "Where does so-and-so, the singer, live?" Or if there was no one in particular that I knew about, I asked: "Doesn't anybody sing in this town?" And I immediately got a response. Only now do I realize how right this was, how

---

[1] I tried to pass myself off as a Spanish newspaperman. I was curious to see if I could get away with it and I figured that as an "exotic" American, I might have trouble getting "inside."

linked to my identity and my destiny. If I was a writer, an artist, then shouldn't I hunt out people who sing, all over the world?

I hit Puerto de Santa María nine o'clock in the morning in the middle of its annual spring fair. The town was slowly waking up and moving, in Sunday-suit array, toward the stock fair. I passed by one of those mangy little bodegas that have as interior decoration barrels of wine and the male voice, and in spite of the early hour I heard some singing. I went in and saw a rough, good-looking, black-haired man with a polka-dot silk scarf around his neck and his arm on a friend's shoulder. They had obviously been going all night and were very high. I ordered a bottle of beer and stood off to one side facing the singer. I don't know how it happened but suddenly we became very close. He must have seen a gesture that told him I both knew and liked what he was singing. Because no one else there did. We exchanged a few words. He was a longshoreman and a disciple of Aurelio Sellés, master of the styles of Cádiz. His tired, serious manner routed any pose and I only told him I was an *aficionado*, but I said it with such pride that he responded immediately and began singing *por soleares*. Fatigue and alcohol cut down his naturally limited resources but the sound was so good: a deep-throated virile *rajo*. Eliseo reminded me of Ángel: someone who has never made it as a pro but who lives as a flamenco more intensely than most professionals. I listened quietly, waiting for him to finish his attempt to impress me and reach inside and pluck out deeper sounds. The friend kept hollering *ole* every five seconds. In the middle of a song, so high he could hardly stand up, Eliseo stopped and said: "Shut up, you know nothing about *cante*." The false *oles* were getting in the way of his search. I could have embraced him. He wasn't a great singer but he was a man in love with his craft. And he was dying from lack of listeners who demanded the best in him. Of the ten or twelve men in the bar, only three were listening and they were more amused than moved. He sang a few more songs but the bar was noisy and he gave it up, agreeing to meet me later. What I heard convinced me that flamenco was not dead in Puerto de Santa María. But I saw that real *aficionados* were just as scarce as in Málaga. As all over.

I went out into the street and drifted with the crowd to the stock grounds. The origins of *feria* are in the buying and selling of stock. The bullfight, singing and dancing, drinking, carnival merriment are off-shoots. I saw a big windy plain and a pathetic sparsity of animals. In the face and figure of an old *gitano* I saw the crumbling structure of the *trato*, the elaborate ritual of stock-dealing—profession, way of life, and artistic arena for the gypsy. In the *trato* the gypsy is a cunning Merlin of a mediator, living from the commission of the sale. To see a gypsy stroke what was yesterday a broken-down, hobbling wreck and is now a smart looking, lively donkey, trimmed to decorative perfection; to see him stroking and livening him up with the point of the cane, running his hand over the beast and saying: "This isn't donkey skin; this is pure silk from Manila!"; to see the pacing back and forth, the examining of the mouth for age, the incessant stream of praise, the leading around of the dazed prospective buyer for the ten wine breaks before the deal is consummated; to hear the swearing, the exclamations, the incredible vocal probing, caressing, stepping back in ancient sense of timing—well, this entire *commedia dell' arte*, made serious by the gypsy's smell and look of hunger and exile, always makes me dizzy and elated, ripe for any adventure, ripe for a few drinks, ripe for some good singing.

I saw this old gypsy standing alone with his cane, the wind blowing through his grey hair, and there was an elegant toughness in his face. I spoke to him and he said to me: "This is finished." "This" referred to the stock fairs all over Andalusia: the machine was removing his prime raw materials. And along with the stock fair go other very important things besides the gypsy and the art of flamenco—the basic ways of behavior, social usages, and attitudes of the countryman, who up to a few years ago shaped most of the Andalusian values. The *feria* was the major event of the year for the farmer. His economy depended on it, he often found a wife there, he released year-long desires, he forgot for a few days the daily back-breaking grind, he revered the patron saint, blood and artistic passions were let loose in the bullfight, relatives and friends were greeted again, romance and satire were expressed in the singing and dancing, and maybe this is why the rural Spanish fairs had and have the feeling of one long pagan orgy—because this moment I don't want to hear about the inevitability of history they come only once a year, whereas the city-dweller may have one any night of the week. *Feria* is now becoming a slightly larger *Sunday in town*: carnival rides for the children, modern dancing for the young with loudspeakers blaring the latest popular music. At as envisioned through the Western concept of progress. I am concerned with what happens to man under change *right now*. I don't know about fifty years hence, but right now the Andalusian countrymen are becoming dazed onlookers, whereas before they were vital participants. What happens to man in the change from participation to passive peripheral watching? I've seen men in the towns where there is no longer any stock fair and the whole *feria* is designed for the young and for the summer vacationers: except for their weather-beaten tanned faces, they have the same look as displaced persons.

And while I'm writing about the disappearance of the traditional fair, it's night, I'm up in the hills sitting outside on the portico. Los Boliches, a suburb of Fuengirola, about two miles away on a straight line, is having its annual fair, and in the transparent night air the sounds are coming through with maddening clarity. Last year I heard the same sounds but fainter: the sound system had not been perfected and there were fewer booths and loudspeakers. But now the chaos of ten or more loudspeakers is hurtling through the megaphone of unobstructed air. A flamenco record rises up, is drowned out by a parody—or is it a serious rendition?—of *Carmen*, followed by a record of insane, helpless male and female laughter; a police siren wails from the carnival rides; three or four lulling suave voices announce products; then versions of pseudo-calypso, pseudo–cha-cha-cha, pseudo-flamenco, pseudo-French, pseudo-Italian, pseudo-rock—all coming in snatches, each momentarily drowning out the other—but dominating everything are the police siren, *Carmen*, and the insane laughter. Jesus! I'm at the foot of the sierra two miles away. Do I have to go up into the caves to escape this sound of dementia?

In Puerto de Santa María, *feria* was more genuine than on the Costa del Sol. Around kiosks selling drinks I watched the youngsters dance to the *fandangos de Huelva* with guitar and fife and drum accompaniment. I was swept into the merriment as singer after singer jumped in, improvising *coplas*:

> *No canto porque me escuchen*
> *ni porque mi voz es buena*
> *canto porque no se junten*
> *la amargura con la pena.*

> I sing not for attention
> Nor because I have a good voice
> I sing to prevent the fusing
> Of bitterness and sorrow.

Everybody was having a good time: foreigners, young, old, *señoritos*, workers, men, women. Those who looked on could still react and comment on the quality of the singing, the dancing, and the verse. No one was excluded and no one was trying to be something else. They were making their own movements. At twilight I left the fairgrounds ready to hear some good singing but Eliseo was nowhere to be found. I headed north towards Seville.

The Roman name for Utrera was *Castra Vinaria,* encampment of wines. One day I'll go back there to see what the town is like. Because the last time I only saw the patio, the smile, and the heart of Fernanda Jiménez, "La Fernanda de Utrera." I entered her house under the pretext of being a reporter making an interview, but I quickly saw that La Fernanda couldn't care less what title I possessed. Her unusual perception told her I was a sincere *aficionado* and that was enough. I looked at that warm wide-mouthed smile, felt the husky voice and the direct glance, and I imagined that a caress from such a woman would make lasting benefits on body and soul. I felt La Fernanda's flame, as person and as artist, immediately, and when I talk about this meeting to people who know her or who have seen a picture of her, they look at me as if I were crazy. They say to me: "She's pretty ugly, though, isn't she?" No, she's not ugly; she's beautiful. Maybe not by tapemeasure statistics or by standards of surface titillation. But if there was a beauty contest based on the touch of fingers, the timbre of the voice, the look in the eye, the smile that surges from contours of the blood and not from toothpaste—La Fernanda would walk away with first prize. Anyway, basking in her warmth, I took my notebook out and jotted down names, dates, details of the rich family history. But I wasn't fooling anyone. If the gypsies of Utrera were no longer on the run, if they now had respectable trades, if they had been incorporated into the Spanish way of life for two hundred years—it didn't matter. All those other centuries of tenuous survival, on the accurate glance, were still very much alive. In the middle of the so-called interview, Mamá, a tall wrinkled woman in her sixties, with a look on her face half Buddha, half Jewish matriarch, erupted: "This man is deceiving us; he's not a poor journalist; he's a rich man; the car he came to town in is his and *you're going to give my girls a fiesta tonight aren't you?"* I mumbled ineffectual protests and La Fernanda came to the rescue: "Hush, Mamá, can't you see this man is here because of his love for *cante?"* This also was a part of La Fernanda's beauty: her ability to read another's inner life. I was proud that a singer of her stature had acknowledged my *afición.*

We met in the evening at a relative's house. They, she and her sister "La Bernarda," were unable to get a guitar; the mood was forced and cold. I was still green in the world of flamenco. A couple of bottles of wine, a relaxed waiting, a little laughter would have eased us into a fuller session. Instead, they never got a chance to warm up. The flamenco setting is so delicate. I compare it to the moment you are going to embrace a woman. If what precedes is conflict, coolness, dissonance, then the moment of touch, the moment of song, will be forced and anxious. In both areas an un-planned, harmonious prologue must take place. That's why, in flamenco, there are actual songs called "songs of preparation" that are a serene, shorter flow before the more dramatic struggle. But even if I felt the brief session was incomplete it didn't matter: La Fernanda *just tuning up* got me excited. With many singers, the preparatory tuning-up, called *temple,* is just a technical clearing of the throat and the finding of the proper tone. But when it's done by a singer like La Fernanda, it is actually the initial search and movement toward the interior; it announces the drama to come. La Fernanda has a small repertory and limited vocal resources, but her *cante* is a pure pilgrimage, her silences so emotional, her echo such a reverberation of ritual: there were just her sister and I in this little room, but even there she had to gather herself in, to concentrate her whole being, and that's what impressed me. Her struggle is not with throat, with melody, with exterior sound—she is submerged in much deeper areas so that even when she fails her near miss is more moving than the performance of singers who are in full possession of their voice and their technique. La Fernanda is the exact opposite of those singers who are content with execution and exact rendering of a given style. If she has not been able to move you, if she has not found her *duende*,[2] her ultimate sound, then she is dissatisfied.

I sat very quietly and listened. I was silent because I felt her struggle and because I did not know enough at that time to fully receive her bare strokes. La Fernanda has inherited the styles of the best singers of Alcalá and Utrera and she only knows how to express them in her own personal way: pure and unadorned. Even to be an *aficionado* is not enough to fully appreciate her singing. One has to be a special *aficionado* and a special human being, because only if you join her in the concentrated search and submersion, only if you let her pull you down into the depths she swims in, can you relish the vitality of her art. I dimly felt this but some nervousness, some fear, prevented me from concentrating; I was lost, and there were no landmarks. I had never been face to face with a singer singing *por soleares* like this and I tried to "remember" instead of drowning myself in the raw present tense. And the crazy thing is that she knew it. She buries her social ego to find her ultimate sound but like all true *cantaores* she is finely attuned to response. When we went back to her house she said teasingly: "Mamá, Pablo liked Bernarda's singing more than mine."

The meeting with La Fernanda not only opened doors for me in the travels that followed; it showed me how much more there was to learn. I had only to mention her name, and the fact that she sang to me, and I was taken into the fold by the better *aficionados*. And she gave me names and places to visit which turned out to be fertile. Which is what her *cante* is: a voyage into magi-

---

[2] See Glossary. For the most penetrating insight into the word *duende* see Federico Garcia Lorca: "The Duende: Theory and Divertissement," an essay in *The Poet in New York* (New York: Grove Press, 1955).

cally fertile human depths. As I said goodbye, the mother, with a
sharp glance set over a demonic half-smile, tossed me a thorny
bouquet: *"Vaya usted con Dios,* and may you have luck to buy
another car."

Alcalá de Guadaira is a small town set in the flat plains about
ten miles southeast of Seville. It was ten in the morning when I
got there and it was already hot. I stepped into a bar off the Plaza
del Duque. The scene: four men intensely playing dominoes, a
woman on her knees washing the floor, an abandoned counter. I
walked over to the counter. Silence was broken only by the venge-
ful *clac* of the dominoes. I told the woman I would like some coffee.
"Miguel," she called to one of the players, "This man wants
coffee." Silence, grunts, and *clacs.* A few minutes passed. I spoke
to the woman again. "Miguel, he wants coffee." An irritated mouth
opened and said: *"You* get him the coffee. Don't you see I'm playing?" The woman sighed, got up, pulled and twisted the knobs
and arms of an espresso machine, which after a minute of hissing,
smoking, and screaming surrendered a small glass of black liquid.
After sipping it for a while, I asked casually, "Can anyone tell me
where Manolito 'él de Maria' lives?" The question took them away
from their game. A small discussion arose. A certain area was mentioned. I told them I was a stranger, and an old man offered his
services. He said he would go to Manolito's house and tell him I
was waiting. I sat down and daydreamed amid the flies and the
static heat. A big, rough looking country boy came in and related
some crime of passion that had happened the night before. A love
betrayal, a father and a son-in-law, a missing horse . . . I couldn't
make it out. After about half an hour the old man came back with
two men, one of them Manolito "él de Maria."

He was a middle-aged man in a battered, pin-stripe suit, a two-
day growth of beard, and a slightly punchy expression due to what
looked like the morning after a heavy night. But when I told him
I had come from his cousin, La Fernanda, to see him, a beautiful
inner spark, like a long, slow, elegant *verónica,* straightened his
worn frame. Once again I played the role of a reporter. And as
always, the interviews carried me where they wanted to go. The
friend, a short, stubby, and staunch supporter of his *compadre*

Manolito, subtly inquired as to the possibility of a few modest banknotes floating into Manolito's pocket from mine. I told them I was not a potential patron but only a poor, humble writer. It was true, but even the little bit of money I had compared to their *sinta*[3] situation made me feel like a lying traitor and I thought of the song:

> *Un pájaro con cien plumas*
> *no se puede mantener*
> *y un escribano con una*
> *mantiene casa y mujer*
> *y querida si tiene alguna.*

> A bird with a hundred feathers
> Can barely keep alive
> And a scribbler with one
> Supports wife and house
> And mistress if he has any.

Money matters among flamencos take on infinite nuances ranging from mandarin insouciance to a blatant "how much." A sense of humor and a sense of theatre are indispensable. In this case the unpleasant shutting of bank doors was softened by my ordering a bottle of wine.[4]

We sat down in a little room, a thin partition dividing us from the domino tournament. We drank wine and munched olives and I let Manolito talk, asking questions only when I felt him lagging. I liked him immediately. He was a flesh-and-blood realization of what excited me most in the world of flamenco: the singer who preserves his purity and his quality, who endures in spite of little or no recognition. The social anarchist in me is at home with those men who refuse to give up a way of being, a way of singing. I equate this with the essential dilemma of choice for all artists: between the refusal to be pulled into the treadmill of art as a commodity and absolute surrender. This is highly nuanced in flamenco. It does not necessarily mean that the *aficionado* is a better or more pure singer than the pro, but that many pros who begin

[3] *Sinta* is slang for *sin tabaco*, "without tobacco," that is, at the lowest economic level.

[4] A bottle of ordinary wine costs twenty cents.

from a solid tradition quickly abandon it for innovations and corruptions of style that seem to please their floating public. Since
all artists would like to live from their art, the pro considers himself
superior because he is "successful." He discounts the fact that he
has to make certain concessions which may finally become inner
ones, concessions that the *aficionado* does not have to make since
money and fame are not working details in his world. Again, the
difference between *artista* and *cantaor* may involve merely a certain
degree of self-confidence, aggressiveness, exhibitionism. I have
never met a flamenco singer who did not have a powerful ego.
What all *must* have, *aficionado* or pro, is *afición*, a pure enthusiasm
for *cante*, which, coupled with a desire to perfect and extend one's
self—and, of course, a natural talent—make for the superior singer.
Without *afición* the singer is a mannequin; he talks about how
much money he's making, his next contract, his erotic conquests;
he gossips about how so-and-so's voice is failing: he talks about
everything except *cante*. If you ask him why he doesn't sing something else besides the same tired *tanguillo*, deformed *bulerías* or
alegrías, he looks sad and says: "It's what the public wants." But
he would be laughed out of a session with serious *aficionados* if
he ever tried to sing *cante jondo*. It's enough for the real *aficionado*
to sing to *one* witness he respects: he needs nothing beyond the
intense focus of a listener who loves and knows what he is doing.

Manolito talked to me about his cousin, Joaquín de La Paula,
great interpreter of the school of Alcalá and a trimmer of donkeys,
as was Manolito's father. He talked to me about relatives and other
great singers of the turn of the century that he knew as a boy.
Names that I had read in books: "Los Cagancho," "El Titi," "La
Pompi," "El Niño Gloria," "Manuel Torres." The wine, the memories, the appreciative listener, began to mount in his spirit. His
wings, drooping from too long a period of oblivion, began to swell.
We left the bar and walked in the baking noonday sun to the
bodega of a friend and sat down in a little room, ordered more wine
and little plates of hot, spiced snails, and closed the door. The
friend softly but directly hinted again at possible payment, a gift,
a needed bill. In the same soft tone I threw sand on his hopes.
Manolito didn't say a word. He lit a cigarette, took another sip of
wine, and started tapping the rhythm of *soleares* on the table.

He *wanted* to sing. He started slowly, working himself into the earth of his art, turning the clods gently, refreshing himself, tuning his body and soul, going back and down and into this music that was his inheritance. It was another sound that told of generations of linked heritage, a sound that came from the blood rather than the throat. But it was tradition *made personal.* I have heard other members of Manolito's family sing the same songs and they didn't sound the same. He saw and sensed my pleasure, and knuckles beating out the rhythm, his body sweating in the airless room, the veins in his neck swelling, his being strained into the more difficult areas and he made a complete *suite por soleares*:

> *Cuando paso por tu puerta*
> *cojo pan y voy comiendo*
> *pa' que no diga tu mare*
> *que con verte me mantengo.*

> When I pass by your door
> I go by eating bread
> So your mother shouldn't say
> That just seeing you I'm fed.

> *Hazme con los ojos señas*
> *que en algunas ocasiones*
> *los ojos sirven de lengua.*

> Make signs with your eyes
> Because sometimes
> Eyes serve as a tongue.

Many singers have said to me, "*Manolito no sabe administrarse.*" He can't govern himself. Meaning, he doesn't take care of himself, he drinks too much, he can't make the fixed schedule of singing jobs. This is all true. It's also true that 90 per cent of the singers working in night clubs in Spain can't sing *por soleares* as authentically, as emotionally, as personally as Manolito "él de María." and so I tell the same story about all these singers. I say the same thing over and over again. If there were a record of the singers mentioned in this book you could put away the words and listen to their sound.

I hitchhiked to Córdoba. There was a three-day festival in honor of "La Niña de los Peines," the greatest female singer of the century. Three nights of the best singers, dancers, and guitarists in Spain. I don't know why, but Córdoba, like no other city in the world, tears me up, pierces my surface, and does something to my eyes so that when I look at objects and people I am constantly wounded: wounded towards love and towards hate. My uneasiness, anger, sadness, loneliness, are sharper in Córdoba. I am shaken by the contrast between the narrow streets of the old quarter with its Moorish imprint and the rich, sleek, uptown streets with the new pastel-colored buildings and stores. The *casino*[5] becomes the *casino* of every town where the merchants and landowners and officials sit and vegetate and digest the huge lunch and the newspapers; digest the stacks of wheat piled on the threshing grounds, the olives and olive oil, the sardines and herrings canned for exportation; they sit and digest, in their four stomachs, the sweat of the farmhand, the laborer, the fisherman. And this that I see all over Spain—why does it wound me so much in Córdoba?

At night and in the burning afternoon I slept in a *posada* where the countrymen still bed down with their horses in the patio. I slept in one century and wandered through the streets of this one. Through the marvel of the Mezquita, through the Judería and its underground synagogue where the Crypto-Jews worshipped (maybe an ancestor of mine was slaughtered there), through the Museo Taurino where the stuffed heads of the bulls with enormous horns and the photos and the lithographs also designated another epoch. This is *always* happening to me in Spain now. Wherever I go I become conscious of past and present. History, a meaningless abstraction for my first thirty years, has become a reality, and if I am obsessed with the past it's only to help me to learn how to act in the present. All I had to do in Spain was open my eyes and I saw the Roman Empire in the form of architecture and law, the Middle Ages in the form of man-woman relationships and in the all-pervasive power of the Church, the twentieth century in the cafeteria, the

---

[5] The *casino* in Andalusia is not a gambling place but the big cafe where the rich hang out in an informal club. In small towns anyone can enter.

machine, and in a new acceleration of the nerves. And these different historical rhythms were all mingling, crashing, screeching, one against the other, some being born and some dying but not wanting to die: like some brave bull with the sword in it, not wanting to go down.

In studying flamenco I read about the history of the Arabs in Spain. Eleven hundred years ago there was a poet named Ziryab who came to the caliph of Córdoba from Baghdad. He was a poet, singer, composer, and guitarist, and it is said he knew twenty thousand songs. Ziryab, among other sages of the Orient, sang in the Mosque of Azzahra where the flower of Cordoban nobility gathered. And here I was in Córdoba where the flower of the contemporary artists and *aficionados* had gathered to pay homage to the century's leading female singer. But in my wanderings I also ran into all kinds of refuse dumps where yesterday's flowers were tossed.

The museum of Julio Romero de Torres, a Cordoban painter now dead, is an intense pictorial cult of woman, and after looking at the whores, virgins, *flamenconas*, represented in his portraits, I watched the same faces sweep by me on the street, some whores, some aristocrats, some working girls: my hunger to embrace them, to speak to them was terrible. I wandered down a narrow street leading to the river and a chubby vulture hissed at me and offered, for a price, some of *her* tired flowers. Córdoba became a crucifix for buried and wound-open feelings and thoughts about Spain. Even the stones were no longer impersonal. I asked a sixteen-year-old boy for directions and he accompanied me, since he had nothing else to do. He was out of work, had been earning 420 pesetas (about seven dollars) a month, full time, in a plastic-bag factory. When I gave him five pesetas for his kindness he turned red with shame and joy. As I crossed the tower-fortress of Calahorra, on the bridge over the Guadalquivir, the walls turned luminous yellow ocher under the streetlight, and as I turned a street near the Mezquita, glimpsing the silver-green trees and feeling the dusty heat lining the river, my solitude sat side by side with the poverty and the frustration in the faces I saw, and I wept furtively on the banks of the river.

The festivals were held in open-air courts and plazas, the prices were popular, and the audience that came was unusual: in their quietness and attentiveness I felt they had come not because it was a part of the *feria* or because it was just a night's entertainment, but because they were passionately interested in the best flamenco. All segments of society were there, from the *señorito* down to the worker with his husky girlfriend on his arm, brimming over with excitement at seeing his idol on the stage and just barely holding himself back from blasting out a thunderous *ole*. But no matter how well organized the whole thing was, no matter how much I realized I was lucky to be able to see, in a few concentrated nights, the best artists, no matter that I made the acquaintance of leading *aficionados*—there was something *artificial* about the whole thing. No one was to blame. It didn't take away from the merit of the event, which was probably the best of its kind, but I couldn't help thinking about Eliseo, about La Fernanda and Manolito "él de La María," about how and where I met them and where they sang to me. I resented the stage and the rows that separated me from the artists. I wanted to be sitting in some tavern, listening to the witty by-play, suddenly hearing someone tune up because he *wanted* to sing and not because it was on the program. But then something happened that drove away all ifs and buts. During the whole night, while excellent singers and dancers had been perform- ing, La Niña de los Peines, in a booth of honor, was off to one side listening silently. Then they persuaded her to sing. She stood there, in a formal dress, an old woman—what had once been a plump, smiling, inimitable *festera*[6] now a body in downward sag— and she sang. The sound was still there, the rhythm etched into her blood, but in a difficult passage her voice cracked and she turned her head in a hot, angry grimace towards her husband as if to say: "Why the hell did I let you talk me into coming here?" But she returned to the song, finished it, and the ovation was end- less. And then, I couldn't believe it, *she danced*! Flamenco dancing is difficult at any age, but Pastora in her late seventies with her warm grace, her movement of arms, the stance of head and neck,

---

[6] A *festera* is a woman who sings the festive styles: *bulerías, tangos, alegrías.*

79

her footwork, obliterated all the previous dancing. I wanted to meet her but there were too many admirers. I told myself I'd meet her in more intimate circumstances, and I left Córdoba.

I hitchhiked back to Málaga. My money was gone and it was time to try and translate all these experiences into words. Near Cádiz, in front of a restaurant, a young, lonely American with a wild beard and a huge bongo drum latched on to me and I thought: Jesus, I'll never get a ride now. But he knew the ins and outs of hitchhiking a hundred times better than I did, and he accosted a man who had just pulled up and who was having coffee. I was just settling into skepticism when out they came, the beard pointing to me and the other man nodding. We climbed into the little four-seater, bongo drum and all. What a trip! Every time we got to a big elegant hotel or restaurant, our benefactor stopped, beckoned to us, we entered, and he was greeted courteously and warmly by the manager and the help; drinks and hors d'oeuvres were put before us, our friend disappeared for a few minutes, then came back and had a drink with us; a soft flurry of farewells, we went out the door and I hadn't seen one peseta requested or handed out. This happened four times. Our mysterious patron was a good-looking, friendly, mustachioed man of about forty-five and I thought maybe he was a big-time smuggler working the coast. It turned out he is the Director of the Government Tourist Office for the province of Cádiz and was on an inspection tour of the hotels and restaurants. I told him a little bit of my story. He is also an *aficionado*, and he promised to usher me into the flamenco environment in Cádiz—we became even friendlier. By the end of the trip I was so mellow that I accompanied him on his inspections, examined the beds and the facilities, inquired about prices for a future stay—what a laugh: one night in one of those beds covered what I needed to live on for a week—joked with the managers, and checked the swimming pools. I was really sorry to see the trip end. I left the Director and my bongo-playing friend in Algeciras and pushed on to Málaga. But I was thinking: maybe I should spend the next thirty years wandering around Andalusia, hunting up *aficionados* and seeing what happens.

What did the trip mean to me? Well, apart from it being a brief course in advanced flamenco studies, it was also the fruit of a year's cultivation that tasted very good. I now had an identity that thrust me immediately into the lives of exceptional individuals, of families, communities, minorities, of the nation itself. One minute I was in a tavern among singers, drunks, parasites, workers, and the next minute I was in the City Hall with the mayor, with poets, philosophers, merchants. I was able to move with ease from individuals to groups. Men I met for the first time gave me their cards and begged me to visit them when passing through their cities. I now spoke a language beyond the learned language. I was no longer drifting through the peripheries of towns and cities, dreaming and consuming myself. I was sitting with men who were singing, drinking, loving, hating. I received their passion and I gave what I was able to give. I no longer lived in a cloud of abstraction called "love for humanity." A man put his arm on my shoulder, sang to me, spoke to me, and I had to respond truthfully. When I speak about the integrity of the *cantaor*, of the need to express the buried center, the buried corners, I'm speaking about the slow transference of these norms into *my* life. And so that's what the trip "meant": it was an extension into a larger world of what had happened to me in the Peña Juan Breva. But such change doesn't happen overnight. I needed another year of solitude, of burning of weeds, of living in the sierra, before I finally broke through and began to put down on paper bits and pieces of that buried center.

7

Manto de rey es mi capa
y corona mi sombrero
mientras las leyes
me las dé yo mismo.

My cape is a king's mantle
My hat a crown
As long as I
Make my own creed.

*R*afael Reyes slipped on his old olive-green
jacket, the brown fedora jaunty no matter how it fell on that East
Indian head, reached for his cane and stepped out into the morning
sun. Antonia was giving suck to grandson Manolito in front of the
old whitewashed stone house surrounded, as in a last stand, by
the new chalets and hotels that were springing up on the beach.
Rafaela came out of a chalet across the way closing her big old-
fashioned cloth bag. "Nada," she said, "words and smiles." They
got out to the highway and walked the half-kilometer to town.
Rafael with that unique gait, a combination of the saunter of the
Parisian flâneur and Trinidadian arrogance: a royalty of movement

accented by the cut of hat and cane. Rafaela with that big-boned shuffle and the prophetic smile softly etched under jutting cheek-bones. Both were thinking: Where is the money for bread coming today? *The woman went to the train station. She was going to Torremolinos to sell cloth. The man eased his sixty-year-old frame into a chair outside of Claro's bar. Maybe someone would want a beast trimmed or there would be a sale. He didn't have the price of a cup of coffee in his pocket.*

The first gypsies I ever knew, way before I was involved with flamenco, were the family of Rafael Reyes in Fuengirola. They consisted of Rafael, his wife Rafaela, two daughters, three sons with their wives, and ten grandchildren. They all lived in one rented house near the beach. Rafael and Rafaela ruled equally as patriarch and matriarch, the man projecting his flamboyant, bare-nerved temperament and the woman her slow, powerful tenacity of worn copper. The two daughters were beautiful princesses, treasured and guarded as potential brides, and they worked obediently at home. When I first came to Fuengirola the eldest son was a *tratante* (stock-dealer), like the father; the two younger sons and the mother sold cloth, "antiques," and whatever else could be materialized out of necessity and imagination. The sons were fallen princes with a raggedy elegance, a pride sometimes desperate, sometimes singing, surging from the blood to the look in the eye and the stance of the body, so that the outer garment, no matter how worn, was impregnated with that pride. The three daughters-in-law lived out their traditional role of bearing children and enduring the daily quest for bread.

The Reyes had only an echo of *gitano grande*[1] about them but it was enough to make them stand out from the other townsmen like poppies in a wheatfield. And it was that difference that made me feel more alive when I was with them. It was like being at the circus watching the magician, knowing his act was a trick but carried into the excitement all the same. I knew they were conning me 75 per cent of the time but it was a *biological* con, a con that was

---

[1] The *gitano grande* is a gypsy who inexorably conserves language, law, art, and custom of the race with an aristocratic dignity and pride that is respected and acclaimed by the sensitive, intelligent *andaluz.*

both the mechanics and the foundation of the race's survival. It was the con of the fairground, and no matter what the theme was, I was always the hick bewitched by the torrent of language and gesture —I was always seeing the broken-down donkey, the drab reality, transformed into a shining, beautiful animal. It was the esthetic laugh-provoking grace of the con that fascinated me. I was impressed by the particular endurance that could make a few words over a glass of wine an unforgettable moment while no one knew where the next meal was coming from. And then, if they made a killing, the day was a pageantry of smiles, new clothes, drink-buying, and Rafael rising to full height, cane over arm, roaring in my face: "There's no one who can sing those songs like me, no one!" And at the same time he'd watch to see if the trousers of his new, striped cocoa-colored suit were falling right over the new boots.

As Fuengirola moved to the peak of its resort prosperity, as the sagging behind of the town exposed itself to the new serums so that the two main industries, farming and fishing, were swallowed up by real estate and construction, the life of the Reyes family changed also. Food prices soared and the daily bullfight for bread, always precarious, became a nerve-wracking struggle. Mechanization and the break-up of farms for real estate cut down the need for beasts of burden, and Rafael's always erratic income diminished along with his meaning in life as a *tratante*. But the great significant change was with the children. For five hundred years the Spanish gypsy despised unskilled manual labor and it was rare for the women to work as servants. But the Reyes family succumbed to economic pressure. The two daughters are maids for foreigners and the eldest son is a construction laborer. To an American this might seem not only insignificant but quite natural. It falls within our social rhythms. Times change and people change with them. But for a people who have endured half a millennium of torture, hunger, persecution—*for the right to remain gypsy*—these changes demolish psychic walls and paint the pride and joy of individualism with the dull grey of mass behavior. The Reyes family are still gypsies. They will not change radically overnight, but already in dress, speech, in an almost imperceptible sag in bearing, in concessions of rooted gypsy law, there is a breakdown:

Otras veces los gitanos
gastaban medias de seda
y ahora por sus desgracias
gastan grillos y cadenas.

Once the gypsies wore
Stockings of silk
And now in evil times
They wear shackles and chains.

In the United States the word flamenco evokes Carmen Amaya, Antonio, and a travel poster showing a gypsy-like dancer in a tight polka-dot dress. We think of flamenco and we think of the gypsies. I shared that popular attitude and thought that it was the gypsies who kept the flamenco heritage alive. I took my first excite- ment and my first knowledge to the Reyes family in the hope they would pull out the aged, heady vintages of their own art. They were gypsies, weren't they? They walked and talked with gypsy grace and Rafael had a hoarse voice that evoked in my frothy imagination the sound of the forge and the *cante por martinetes.* I took advantage of a "Pablo-we-consider-you-one-of-the-family" street meeting with all the beautiful vocal swirls that are sincere and a con at the same time, and I brought some choice records to their house. In a short time I realized they knew very little about flamenco. I was surprised, but I thought: Wait; you're still the outsider; maybe on more intimate occasions they'll show you another deeper side. I went to christenings and I went to the wedding of María, the eldest daughter, where family intimacy was at its highest and relatives came from the provinces of Córdoba and Málaga. But nothing changed. They all danced their little *tanguillo* with more or less piquant grace but no one, save Antonia, one of the daughters-in-law, was capable of singing any style completely. Antonia, eyes so scornful that when the rare smile came it was a fragrant spice, was the only one with tangible sub- stance of *gitana grande* and she sang *por bulerías* with a deep- voiced gypsy echo. No matter how much pleading and begging went on, she only sang when she felt like it and more than once she remained mute the entire evening. Singing was not entertain- ment for her. It was a surrendering of her inner self and she couldn't do it lightly or with strangers. Rafael sang bits and pieces of songs, his voice gone—he had a wonderful sound, and who knows, maybe in some wild inspired dawn he would have remembered the great singers of his youth but it never seemed to happen.

With further study my surprised disappointment dissolved. I began to discover that although flamenco has its roots in folk music, it is really a refining, a stylizing, of those roots by individual artists who perform for a reduced minority. Most Andalusians, gypsy or not, know very little about it nor are they very concerned about it. I began to understand that flamenco has always been in the hands of the professional artist, the semi-professional, and the dedicated *aficionado*.

Legend, literature, theory, prejudice—all blur the gypsy reality and dress it in picturesque or enigmatic clothes. Actual contact strips away a great deal of the confusion. Whether he is fairly integrated to non-gypsy society or whether he perpetuates his own traditional customs, the gypsy is always conscious of his racial origins and always fiercely proud of being gypsy.

In Spain, bands of gypsies were first noted in the province of Catalonia around 1450.[2] Though they wandered all over the peninsula, the majority finally chose the fertile sunny region of Andalusia as a camping ground. Like all nomads they despised agriculture and manual labor. The women sold petty wares, told fortunes, begged, sang and danced. The men sold and traded horses and beasts of burden and were metal-workers. The Zincali, or "black men from the Sind," an area in northern India, found in Andalusia reflections of their original oriental life: in climate, landscape, music, and in a people whose blood carried many eastern strains. As in the rest of Europe, the Spanish gypsies were severely punished for thievery and for refusal to enter organized society. In every century, some malevolent thinker, clergyman, or statesman called them "children of the devil" and erected laws to end their nomadic ways. Inefficiency and provincial separatism prevented the

[2] There is a theory that different gypsy tribes entered Spain through North Africa at an earlier date, that they were more sedentary and that they settled in lower Andalusia.

enforcement of such laws, and the gypsy remained nomadic until the end of the eighteenth century. For three hundred and fifty years he clung to his own unwritten law, which read: "Befriend the gypsy; deceive the non-gypsy." He lived according to the rhythms of his nature and within a powerful impulse to be his own master. Then, in 1783, in the reign of Charles III, another law was passed that forbade him to use his own language and to wander through the countryside. But the same law offered unusual opportunities for employment and gave the gypsy the same rights before the law as the Spaniard. The beginning of the nineteenth century saw the slow conversion of the gypsy nomad to a more or less sedentary citizen who lived in gypsy quarters in the Andalusian towns and did not intermarry, who took up the trades of fishmonger, bootblack, slaughter-house man, innkeeper, in addition to the traditional vocations of smith and stock-dealer. In 1841, George Borrow, the English literary adventurer, wrote the words of an old gypsy: "The king's law has finished off the gypsies." But even now, a hundred and twenty-five years later, when the number of families who wander around on foot, burro, or by battered caravan has greatly diminished, even in those who *seem* to have succumbed —the shoeshine boys, the lottery vendors, the old *tratantes* sitting idle, cane crooked over arm for hours on end—if you sit with them for a while you will realize it's taking a little longer to make the gypsy conformist and anonymous.

The world of flamenco is split by controversy over the exact contribution of the gypsy. At one extreme stand those who attribute everything to the *gitanos*, and at the other, those who claim the gypsy brought nothing, borrowed everything, and, in addition, is also responsible for most of the adulterations. The truth lies somewhere in between.

Only the Andalusian sings flamenco, whether gypsy or not. From the eighth through the fifteenth centuries Andalusia was dominated by Islam. And as one of many caliphates, it exchanged musical influences with Arabia, Syria, Persia, Morocco, and Turkey. In spite of the expulsion of the Moors from Spain at the close of the fifteenth century, many remained tucked away in the small hill towns in every Andalusian province. The gypsy nomads, horse-traders, fortunetellers, and smiths came into contact with the *moriscos*. There is a definite kinship between the primitive flamenco forms (*cante jondo*) and the music of the Orient. In the *siguiriya gitana*, the major style of *cante jondo*, always dominated by gypsy singers, we can hear this kinship.

Until the emergence and growth of the *café cantante*, from 1860 on, the primitive styles were scarcely known. Whether they created these styles or not, the gypsies have always been their great interpreters. Both in music and verse, the primitive songs express secretive, sacred, ritualistic qualities. This is why it is thought they are the deep expression of a persecuted people. A major catalyst in the growth of the *café cantante* was the art and personality of a non-gypsy singer, Silverio Franconetti, whose teachers were gypsies, and who wanted to lift the gypsy art from the obscurity of the tavern into the more respectable air of the music hall. Silverio opened an important *café cantante* in Seville around 1880. In the *café cantante* the ritualistic essence of flamenco was lost, but the gypsy and the Andalusian singer alternated freely and there began the mixing, borrowing, transforming, broadening, and stylizing that takes place when an exclusive art form steps into commercial surroundings. At the same time, flamenco expanded from its nursery of lower Andalusia and extended over the whole of Andalusia; many new forms were created, some derived from the primitive *jondo* styles and others from regional folk forms.

Individual ways of singing depend on the vocal instrument, psychic temperament, imitative sources, and environmental influences. Among the gypsies themselves, one from Cádiz will sing differently than his cousins in Seville and Málaga. It is true that most gypsies prefer certain *stylistic vocal traits* within the vast flamenco repertory and this preference is what is commonly called *cante gitano*.

> In *cante gitano*, the *melisma*[3] is less used; on the other hand, frequent syncopations that tear the rhythm and beat it, giving it the air of a hiccup of weeping, are employed. The note, instead of prolonging itself, is interrupted, amputated in a violent and

[3] A *melisma* is a note or notes sustained and extended over a given syllable.

painful silence, full of frustrated utterances that are a pathetic underlining of expression. It is said that the gypsies "bite" cante.[4]

But this hiccup of weeping, called *jipío*, can only convey the sensation of weeping *when the singer really feels it*: otherwise it becomes an empty device. Many non-gypsy singers use it and use it well. What is true is that in the last third of the nineteenth century, new flamenco forms emerged that were radically different from the *jondo* styles, and in general the gypsy did not take to them as, for example, the *malagueña*, the country *fandangos*, and the styles of *levante*. The long, delicate melodic line, the free rhythm of these songs, were almost diametrically opposed to the dense substance and fixed beat of, for example, the *soleares* and the *siguiriyas*, favorite styles of gypsy singers. Notable exceptions, again dependent on place of birth and vocal instrument, defy these general classifications, but during the 1963 contest in Málaga I had a good chance to observe the basic factors in play. The contest centered around the *malagueña* and derivative styles. After hearing a variety of voices, all non-gypsy, interpret more or less faithfully the delicate melody and formal structure of the *malagueña*, two professional gypsies, not from Málaga, thrust some strange dramatic notes into the proceedings. Both had raw, hoarse voices and short-breath deliveries with subtle but important differences. "El Chaqueta" had a hoarseness like that of a bull-calf and he sang the *malagueña* with a soft half-smile on his face as if he were aware of its delicate beauty, but it was sheer anguish to endure his hoarse-voiced strained attempt to sustain the *melisma* and end the melodic line properly. His spirit was a garden pool of the Alhambra, but his voice was like Wallace Beery's. The other singer, "El Pili," used his hoarseness as a club, attacked the *malagueña* with a defiance and a sinister melodramatic loudness, and the *melisma* came out like Bert Lahr. There is no music with such infinite space for individual variations as flamenco, but the essential emotional and formal structures of a given style cannot be deformed. The

[4] From Carlos y Pedro Caba, *Andalucia: Su comunismo y su cante jondo* (Madrid: Biblioteca Atlántico, 1933).

flowing essence of the *malagueña* cannot be rendered by a hoarse voice with a thick vibrato nor, on the other hand, can the raw anguish of the *siguiriya* or the *martinete* be told by a sweet tenor.

The gypsies, then, have a predilection for certain styles and stylistics which are passed down from one generation to the other, and they perform these in preference to others. But it is inaccurate to limit them to one way of singing flamenco. This is easily demonstrated by listening to different gypsy singers performing the same style. The sound, the attack, the psychic result, are all varied. Again, more important than race are the vocal instrument, temperament, and environmental sources.

The gypsy is born into an elaborate setting of histrionics that he develops and plays on every day of his life in the search for bread, and he shifts from lament to mockery with such ease that the outsider is easily taken in. With the evolution of flamenco into its conscious folkloric phase, the gypsy has allowed himself to be exploited in a banal, vulgar display for the easy money that comes with tourism. But it is to be remembered that this is within a general thirty-year decadence (the period 1920 to 1950) promoted and sustained by non-gypsy artists. One of the major factors in the commercial exploitation was the rise of dance to first place in the flamenco hierarchy. The gypsy, always dominating the dance scene, moved easily into the false merriment and tinsel picturesqueness that characterize the mechanical performance for tourists. The *calés* have a special talent for the rhythmic percussive accompaniment that includes handclapping, finger-popping, heel-and-toe tapping, timely vocal utterance—all of which build theatrical atmosphere and fit well in commercial settings. And so the image of the theatrical *cuadro flamenco*, composed of gypsies, spread throughout the world as the typical flamenco image. The fireworks of flashy dancing and slick accompaniment replaced the pure emotion of the song.

There is nothing more beautiful and more difficult than a series of *bulerías* sung, danced, and accompanied in a unity of intermoving parts. This seemingly light festive form contains an unusual richness and is a synthesis of various styles and emotions that range from festive play to anguish, from serious defiance to lyrical frivolity—all within the two-minute breadth of the song. When only one facet, the festive gaiety, for example, is emphasized, the impact is thin. In flamenco, vulgar performances often stem from a scorn or mistrust of the artist towards the spectator. The authentic flamenco, gypsy or not, will rarely give everything he has before a lay audience, whether in a glamorous night club or an intimate back room. The gypsy of any serious rank jealously guards the treasure of his art, which he believes stems from the "trunk of Pharaoh," and will only reveal it to the *payo* (non-gypsy) who has won his friendship, his respect, and his trust. The rest of the time he offers the rind.

This attitude of the gypsy as high priest of an art created and understood only by his own race was displayed on one of those rambling, dispersed nights when flamencos get together and some dramatic flare-up of temperaments in the early morning hours illumines the flamenco psyche. The event was of heightened interest because it began in the official milieu of a government-sponsored lecture-hall attended by intellectuals, businessmen, and local officials and their families, and it ended in the mangy setting of a workers' bar. The lecture, by Ricardo Molina, Cordoban poet and flamenco authority, was on the gypsy's role in flamenco art and it was being illustrated by one of the leading gypsy singers, Antonio Mairena. Molina's words, backed by Mairena's deep gypsy *rajo*, inflamed the Malagueñan intellectuals, who attacked Mairena, Molina, and the theory that the gypsies are a cornerstone of flamenco art. Afterwards, I and some other *aficionados* lured Mairena and Molina to Augustin's kiosk in the Plaza de la Merced. Mairena was Augustin's idol; he was so excited to meet him in person and he put on all his Mairena records. The wine started to flow, we listened to records of other old-time gypsy greats, and we all thought that Mairena had calmed down and had forgotten the previous attack in the lecture-hall. We were wrong. An hour later we were still hoping he would break out into song when some little flurry of conversation set him off and he exploded. "You can't feel what I'm singing. Not you, nor you, nor you. Nobody here can feel it in his soul. You're not gypsy." And he walked out. Though this is a common attitude of the gypsy artist, each one plays with it, conceals or blatantly displays it, according to the mood, the circumstance, and the trust and respect he has for the witness.

Facing the ruins and the gardens of the Alhambra in Granada is the hill of the Sacromonte where the gypsies live in caves built into its side. Nine-tenths of the inhabitants go through banal motions of flamenco art for the constant stream of tourists from all nations. I didn't think it possible for genuine flamenco to exist there. Then I went up with a friend, Fernando Montoro, who was studying at the University of Granada, who knew the city well, and who was an intense, practicing *aficionado*. But we didn't go to the caves. He took me to one of the bordering *ventas*. The *venta* is a roadside inn which stays open all night; singers and guitarists hang out there; you can hire them, go into a private room and order wine and food. In just such a *venta*, only a few doors away from the neon-lit caves, I met Juanillo "El Gitano." Fernando had sung with Juanillo before, there was a good relation between them, and so it wasn't a cut-and-dried buying of entertainment. Juanillo had knocked around Málaga for a few years, he knew Diego, and we talked about mutual friends. We sipped wine, chatted, and eased slowly into the music. He needed no coaxing. He took his guitar out of the case and leaned over it, without histrionics, just a man in love with his instrument and his art and very happy that people were listening appreciatively. He alternated with Fernando and for a few moments there was a clear father-son current between this old gypsy and the young chemistry student. They sang *soleares*, *bulerías*, and later, *alboreás*, the gypsy wedding song. At one or two in the morning, when everyone was hungry, two fried chickens cooked in garlic and olive oil were brought in, and our host, a young *granadino*, topped these off with canned peaches in thick syrup. Red Valdepeñas wine kept the hearth-fires going. Juanillo "El Gitano" was not a famous singer or guitarist, but the love for his music lit up his Mongoloid face and his smile touched everyone in the room. He sang purely, with no false gestures, no gypsy theatricality. The world of flamenco abounds with such super-egos that most sessions suffer from tense or petulant conflicts. But this evening was a tender communion between the need to express and the need to receive that expression. Juanillo shaped the evening but we all shared in it.

Perhaps both he and Antonio Mairena feel that anything or anyone that doesn't stem from the "trunk of Pharaoh" has little value in flamenco art, but being less a *maestro* and more a modest singer, he, Juanillo, doesn't thrust this attitude in your face. In the world of flamenco each singer expresses the larger attitudes within the nuances of his individual psyche.

> *Hambre de gitano*
> *como sed de perro*
> *ninguna se rabia.*
>
> A gypsy's hunger
> Like a dog's thirst:
> Neither maddens.

Like the *andaluz*, the gypsy is a traditionalist, in family life, tribal customs, vocational patterns, sex. But he lives within a tremendous dualism of the tribe and the world. He elaborates a different set of social gestures to move and survive in that outside world. The greatest factor in the break-up of gypsy patterns is mechanization and modern progress which is cutting away his connection to rural life. This has been going on slowly for a long time but in the last ten years the process has been accelerated. Last year, the gypsy nomad, drifting through Fuengirola, camped out in any one of the several vacant lots at the edges of town. This year, a bowling alley, a hotel, a housing project, stand on those lots. There are fewer donkeys to sell, to shoe, to trim. The plastic bag replaces the hand-woven basket. So the gypsy sells cloth. But in a few years, the factory-made garment will be much cheaper in Spain than the tailor-made one, and another door will be closed. The gypsy will go the way of the *andaluz*. He'll become a factory-worker, a construction-laborer and, later on, a clerk. Up to now he has not allowed the new social and economic ways to change him. He is still the great traditionalist absorbing the new gadgets into the temperament and attitudes of his race. Wealth does not modify him but rather makes him more intensely extravagant: more gypsy. Like Rafael Reyes or his sons when they make a killing. But the gypsy is also an *andaluz* carried to extremes. It's impossible to live five centuries as a social and psychological outcast and not be extreme. It's impossible to hold as the highest value the freedom to live out one's laws and not be extreme. It's impossible to be dressed in rags, to sleep in any vacant lot, never knowing where the next meal is coming from, and yet have an unshakeable pride in one's blood, one's race, one's self—and not be extreme. In a country where the norm is work ten hours a day six days a week, to defy this norm, to live in dreams, in a lubricant tongue, by the wife's selling cloth—is to be extreme. How long will this last? I don't know, but I feel that no matter how modern and industrialized Andalusia becomes, there will always be a few gypsies on the outside, quietly laughing at the organized hustle and bustle, camping a little farther from town because the outskirts will have spread, but going about their daily con, *as always*, and then moving on.

More than the average *andaluz*, the gypsy still conserves fragments of his flamenco heritage. Even though it is, more often than not, an inferior, adulterated brand, no other music will be sung or danced at a gypsy *fiesta*. This is not true of the Andalusian *fiesta* where the international ballad, the fox trot, latin music, rock-and-roll, the twist, now predominate. But with both groups, *cante jondo* is the patrimony of a select few. There are also gypsies without *afición*. The gypsy sings and dances flamenco because in it he finds the whole gamut of expression that tells the sorrows and sufferings, the joys, the mocking, defiant attitudes of the race. Whether what he is singing is gypsy in origin or whether he stresses certain stylistic devices is not of transcendent importance. Whether or not he is truly feeling what he sings *is*.

8

Er dinero es un mareo
aquel que tiene parné
es bonito aunque sea feo.

Money makes you dizzy
He who has it
Is handsome though he's ugly.

*T*he first national flamenco contest was held
in Granada in 1922. Manuel de Falla, Federico García Lorca, and a
host of other poets, painters, musicians, and thinkers were among
the organizers. In a pamphlet accompanying the rules of the contest they set down their aims:

The Artistic Center of Granada, realizing the importance that the
conservation of its primitive songs has for the artistic life of a
country, has organized the present contest for the purpose of
stimulating the cultivation of these old songs, in many areas
almost completely forgotten. The Contest . . . has as its aim the
"renaissance, conservation, and purification" of the ancient *cante
jondo* . . . which, poorly esteemed and misunderstood by people

today, is considered an inferior art, being, on the contrary, one of the worthiest popular artistic manifestations in Europe.[1]

The contest was held in the Alhambra, no professionals were allowed, and an old man named Diego Bermúdez, from Morón de la Frontera, won first prize. But no one followed up this first effort until thirty-four years later, and in the interim the whole body of flamenco suffered a decline and corruption.

In 1956, a group of men in Córdoba, backed financially and spiritually by an unusual mayor, organized the second contest.[2] Some ripe turning in the sensibility of a minority, a few serious authors and record companies working independently but simultaneously, brought about a renovation. And so the contest acted as a projectile, set up important norms, and now stands as a landmark in the renaissance. Two important factors coincided happily. One, the organizers were exceptional *aficionados*, free and able to act only in the interest of pure *cante*, and two, there had been built up, in the thirty-four years between the two contests, a small body of authentic singers for whom such an event was an Eden in the long, lonely endurance amid the more successful commercializations. The directors of the Cordoban contest tried to suffuse every detail with the warm pulse of flamenco norms. They tried to create an atmosphere that would encourage spontaneity. They knew that in order to arouse the emotional depths of a singer, the supreme factor in flamenco, the setting had to be human. They stressed *cante* rather than *contest*. They were interested in encouraging young singers and crowning those old-timers who had kept the pure forms alive. And they succeeded.

By 1962 the flamenco contest was clearly an ascending phenomenon, and I made the rounds of the major and minor ones: Vélez Málaga, Jerez, de la Frontera, Córdoba, San Roque, Málaga. Although in each there were positive achievements, the previous aims were being buried under a scramble for the ever increasing prize money, for local prestige, touristic promotion, for prettifying and animating a fair with something typical. It's true that new

[1] Translated by the author from *Primer concurso de cante jondo* (Granada: Editorial Urania, 1922).

[2] Described magnificently by Anselmo González Climent in *Cante en Córdoba* (Madrid: Escelicer, 1957).

singers were revealed, that a general interest in classical flamenco
was revived, that important records were produced, but it was too
much like the fireworks at these fairs: a brief moment of startling
beauty and then disappearance. A real rebirth can occur only when
something is born within the participants that they will carry to
other people and places, when a free exchange of art and ideas
takes place. The flamenco contest was becoming a crepe-paper
rainbow with everybody running for the real pot of gold. The old
Spanish separatism, the narrow provincialism, was still very much
alive: each town clamored for the fat share of the glory and
prestige and too often the delicate inner structures of singer and
song were forgotten.[3] I had a good chance to observe all this when
Fuengirola followed suit, planned a contest during its annual fair,
and I was asked to be a member of the jury.

I was scared. I knew I had so much more to learn about the
technical intricacies, the regional and personal variations, the exact
traditional renderings. My knowledge could pass in a private session but in a public contest the responsibility was heavy. But I
had no fear of intuiting what was for me more important: how
much of the flamenco drama the singer was living and how much
of it he could communicate. I knew I could tell whether he was
singing from his head or from his heart and soul. I didn't relish
being stuck onto an official perch, but I knew the experience would
be valuable. I would be able to view all the workings of a contest
from the inside, and I dreamed of meeting new singers and of
being involved in exciting private sessions. It had been frustrating
to attend the other contests as a spectator, knowing that the showy
public finale was just a crust compared to the deeper, fruity
dimensions of the preliminaries, the private dialogues, the discussions, the nighttime *juergas* for a select few. And I was flattered
that they thought me good enough. I accepted.

> *La naturaleza humana*
> *según en sus hijos veo*
> *parió gigante el deseo*
> *y u la posesión enana.*

---

[3] The more local contests of Vélez Málaga and San Roque were not involved
in this race for prestige.

> Human nature
> As I see it in its children
> Made desire a giant
> And possession a dwarf.

Ninety-nine per cent of the people of Fuengirola knew nothing and cared less about flamenco. But the town vibrated with its sounds. From the stock-fair in the eucalyptus grove to the carnival rides on the beach, from the swankiest café to the smallest candy-booth, any merchant who had a phonograph was playing flamenco. And everybody was talking about it. The loudest hubbub centered on the 86,000 pesetas ($1430) awarded as prize money. Even on the Costa del Sol, where construction-workers received the highest wages in Spain because of the high demand for labor, it took a skilled mason or carpenter fifteen months and a farm laborer about two and a half years to earn that much money. So the open-mouthed reaction was justified. Apart from the money, they talked about their favorite idols: the pretty-voiced singers of the *fandanguillo* in vogue these past forty years. Only the real old-timers had heard classical flamenco and that in Málaga before the Civil War—men like my neighbor, Pepe Santaella, who carted grapes to the capital, walking the twenty miles behind a mule or a donkey, having to spend the night waiting for the early-morning market, would go to the Café Chinitas to hear the great singers, watch the girls dance, and laugh at the comics. For the Fuengirola young, flamenco was an old-fashioned, sad sound. They were busy learn-ing the *"tuis."*

The preliminaries of the contest were held on two nights in a private salon in the City Hall. We were to choose finalists who would then compete publicly in the brand new movie-house in a spectacular grand finale with radio broadcast and all. The windows of the salon looked out on a little plaza where tables from the fishermen's bar across the street had been set up. The plaza was packed with people who hoped to hear some of the singing through the open windows. Inside, the proceedings unfolded as if the men who came in were being tried for a crime. We, the jury, sat at a table replete with wine and *tapas*. A guard opened the door; in came the singer; he was given a quick glass of wine, a few seconds to check his tone with the guitarist, and presto—sing! When he finished, nobody said a word. Then exit singer. I remember one young boy who, scared to begin with, turned pale at the setting in the salon and couldn't free himself of his fear all the way through the song. Everything I had ever experienced in the true flamenco medium rose up to yell one long loud protest. But I was chained. The moment I became a part of the group in authority I was forced to accept their rules. I kept silent, poured myself another glass of wine, and listened to the singing. I was angry. It would not have been difficult to create a more relaxed atmosphere. Except for fear. The fear imposed by the 86,000 pesetas, by the fact that it was the first contest for the jury as well as the singers and several members were insecure about their knowledge, were uneasy that maybe they were in over their heads. In order to mask this fear they set up severe business-like methods and maintained a rigid gravity. On the second night this gravity was revealed in its shallowness and inadequacy. Diego had been invited to sit with the jury as guest of honor, and on hearing a line he liked he let out an *ole*. Several jury members tried to shush him and he said: "I can't help it. I'd burst if I couldn't say *ole* when I felt like it." It was a critical bull's eye. The atmosphere was totally anti-flamenco. Without spontaneity of singer and listener and in the *atmosphere* itself, there can be no authentic flamenco. In a contest this is difficult: without some order it would be a never ending chaotic circus. But only flamenco canons should dictate this order; if the jury is free, secure, and spontaneous, it will reflect directly on the looseness of the singers, especially when they are *aficionados* unaccustomed to public singing. So my dream of a rich preliminary session was quickly shattered. But, as usual, individual singers consoled me in my disgruntlement with the group.

There were eighteen contestants but two really stood out. One who lost, eliminated the second day, and the other who won a first prize. The loser, Juan "El Lucentino," looked like a certain character actor, I can't remember his name, who always played the stoolie, the gangster, the night clerk. He always took a beating or was killed. I remember him in the Humphrey Bogart pictures: a little man with a soft, almost cultured voice. "El Lucentino," nervous in a cheap, ill-fitting suit, emitted the mental aroma of someone who has never made it. His singing was uneven, he lost the beat at times, his endings were weak, but *he sang with feeling* and he struggled with the song. This was to happen so many times during the contest. Singers with beautiful voices, perfect execution, left me completely cold. And some nervous, insecure singer stirred me. "El Lucentino" wasn't good enough to make the finals but *he was more flamenco* than others who did, and he deserved more than cold silence. He was to receive open response somewhere else. The day before the finals I was sitting in my friend Danny Swerdloff's house when he came in, excited and a little high: "I just had a crazy experience in Tirita's bar. There were a couple of flamenco singers from the contest there and they both were singing. One was a man with a powerful voice, with a lot of admirers and parasites around him, I think he made the finals, but somehow he didn't convince me. He sang with a lot of weeping sounds, and as he finished he made some wisecrack and ordered drinks for everybody. It was an act. But this little guy, the other one, started singing to me—you know I don't know anything about flamenco—but he made me believe him. I mean he *made* me because at first I was embarrassed. Here was this guy singing his heart out to me who knows nothing about flamenco, but I was cornered; there was nothing to do but look at him and listen and I liked what he was singing and told him so. He was eliminated and doesn't have money to get back home so he's trying to pick up change singing in the bars. And do you know what he tells me? 'Only the *americano* liked me.' He didn't know I was your friend and I didn't say anything to him."

It was true: Danny knew nothing about flamenco and for a year I had been relating my experiences to him, working out my ideas and theories. He had listened, enjoying some of it, coasting with the rest, but only now did he understand what it was all about. Only when "El Lucentino" sang directly to him and he became personally involved in the flamenco drama did it have meaning for him. And it was curious that it happened with a *cantaor* who will always be a tavern-singer: a singer *who must sing* and who only needs a little wine and an appreciative listener to get him going. "El Lucentino" will not win prizes in flamenco contests but he will kindle and stir the feelings of a lot of men in a lot of bars. Sometimes his singing will be maudlin and sometimes finely etched, but with him flamenco leaves the theatre, the contest, the stage, and returns to one of its early haunts:

> *No canto porque me escuchen*
> *ni porque suene mi voz*
> *me lo manda un amiguito*
> *y no le digo que no.*

> I sing not to be heard
> Nor to display my voice
> I sing because a friend asks me
> And I can't tell him no.

I sat there listening to the different singers, jotting down impressions, and in came a little wiry man radiating a nervous energy that was painful, comic, and tender all at the same time. He sparred awkwardly with the guitarist for a few minutes in an attempt to find his proper tone and when he began singing, *por soleares*, my initial sympathy deepened and memory focused to a precise time and place: I had met him before. It was at a banquet thrown by the Terry distillery at the contest of Jerez de la Frontera in the spring of 1962. The flamencos had just polished off a huge table with all kinds of delicious hors d'oeuvres and the great dry sherry wine of the house, and no sooner had we finished eating than this little man, his face a wine-inspired color, said: "Well aren't we here to sing?" And he let out with a *siguiriya*. This was the way I'd first met Manuel Ávila and the way I'd last seen him: singing. He hadn't wanted to impress anyone. *He just had to sing.* The other singers had laughed at his inability to contain himself, but his need to sing was beyond any laughter, whether affectionate or derisive. I realize now that he hadn't been drunk on the wine but on the reality that for three days and nights in Jerez he was breathing and pulsing *cante*, that just to be near so many singers and so many guitars was enough to get him high and he was going to take in and give out as much as he could because afterwards he would have to return to his hilltown in the province of Granada, to his farm and his butcher shop and smolder for a long while until he could escape and explode again. He did the same thing in Málaga in the 1963 contest. The rest of the singers were saving their voices for the finals, but he was singing from the moment he got up, in private and public *juergas*, singing without sleep until the early hours of the next morning, and of all the singers he was the only one the audience called back for more applause. He wasn't wasting his seed: it was stored up so long that it came out tireless and endless.

I had wanted to talk to him in Jerez but there were so many distractions, so many singers, that I lost him in the crowd. But here he was again with that deep open-throated, open-hearted sound that broke through to the feelings like the sun after days of rain. Manuel Ávila is a curious flamenco singer. He listens to himself, shaking his head in disapproval, making horrible grimaces, but it's not a cold self-listening in order to achieve a perfect technical rendition, because the emotional sparks he gives off touch everyone. He simply is not sure of himself in public; he has sung so rarely outside of his town, Montefrío, he has sung so little with a guitar, that he checks himself constantly for mistakes. But he *cares* so much that you have to react. I have never seen anyone indifferent to his singing. Some are impressed, some are enfolded in it, and some laugh. The transparency of his love and his struggle is so great that many cannot repress a nervous titter. They are so used to people locking up and masking their feelings that this vulnerability astounds them and makes them laugh. The same thing that has happened with Diego has happened with Manuel Ávila: their sound coincides with the best of their being, and they may lack physical strength or technical knowledge but the full sound is there, and in their tuning up you are already excited and expectant. I knew all too well that such a man was rare and I sought him out, contest or no contest, juryman or not. He was competing in three of the four categories and made the finals easily.

What was the difference between Ávila and "El Lucentino," two singers who approached *cante* nervous and insecure? Among other things, "El Lucentino" carried a piece of his fear with him while he sang and this fragmented his sound, but Manuel Ávila, though painfully struggling, left the fear and the awkwardness behind in the preceding silence. He was a man walking in the sierra against a powerful wind· but he was climbing steadily. From the first moment I heard and saw Manuel Ávila I felt an unusual sympathy for him, and after forming a friendship, after spending time with him, I began to realize that he was the living symbol of why flamenco had lured and held me for more than five years. Now, whenever I use the words *afición, pure, spontaneous*—I see his face. I know one thing: flamenco survives because of the few Manuel Ávilas scattered throughout Andalusia. And I know I will seek him out again and again.

The finals began at eleven and ended at four in the morning. Pepe Luque and Pepe Navarro were also on the jury and the men of the Peña came as spectators. I was so used to seeing them in Málaga, on the street corners and in the known bars, that it was strange to run into them here. Across the way from the theatre there was a little bodega doing a booming business. Most of the singers were in there trying to ease their nerves and it was funny and sad at the same time to see them trying to reach that mellow state in such a short, artificial time. I became so involved chatting and drinking with them that I got to the theatre late: the contest had already begun.

The jury sat backstage screened off from the public but with a side view of the singers. Among the thousand gestures, events, and memories, I remember particularly the singing of Augustin "El Gitano," a big, powerful gypsy who started his song a tone too high and finished it on sheer guts, the singing of Manuel Ávila and of "El Niño de las Moras," a seventy-five-year-old gnome from Málaga who sang the *taranta*. All three won first prizes in their respective categories. The fourth memory is myself opening bottles of Fino La Ina, the delicious dry sherry bottled by Pedro Domecq. I don't remember how or why I got the job but I was opening bottles all night. The rest of the singing was post-climactic compared to the preliminary sessions. A stage seems and is artificial to the true listening *aficionado* and with the microphone and the radio announcer, the applause, the screened side view, the hasty jotting down of points, the counts and re-counts, the constant alternating between corkscrew and pencil for a moment I thought the contest was taking place in Sammy's Bowery Follies. Pepe Navarro, high to begin with, proceeded to get stoned into a languid, sleepy state broken by raw comments on almost everything and ear-to-ear grins directed at me. "You're all right, Pablo," they seemed to say. "You're still enjoying the singing in spite of all the manure that surrounds it." He was bored. After forty years of listening to flamenco, this small-town contest with a dearth of exceptional singers was lulling him to sleep. But he kept reviving with the help of La Ina. And then when Manuel Ávila began singing the *serrana* (Pepe Navarro had not attended the preliminaries) I saw him lift his head as if to say: "What's this mountain flower doing here amid the tinfoil and refuse?" And the public reacted the same way. Ávila is a unique case of a singer who operates so much more fully in the closed-door session yet is still able to excite a profane audience. In contrast to the slickness of the professional singers his free, open, fierce sound obliterated the theatrical setting and his pure vulnerable giving of self stirred his listeners. For a brief moment he made them remember the ancient roots of this music.

The contest ended; the prizes were awarded; the last bottle of La Ina was drunk. We sat outside under the awning of the Casino, tired, but hoping that some private session would jell. But the prize-winners had all disappeared and the bars were no longer serving. There was a sour aroma of disappointment in the air. Like those nights at the Peña when there was more uninspired speech than singing and the last sip of wine tasted bad. I left and went to sleep. I found out later that they had kept going, found some more wine somewhere, Pepe Navarro had sung all over the place, the elastic on his undershorts broke and he lost them. They finally got him back to Málaga on the eight A.M. train. Again I had made a mistake. I should never have left Manuel Ávila's side. I *know* he was singing somewhere.

Fuengirola continued its frenetic rhythms of *feria*. The following evening the regional dance group from the Sección Femenina de Coros y Danzas of Málaga was announced. It was to take place at the official pavilion at eleven o'clock. We got what was probably the last table and grimly endured pushing, toe-stepping, no service, and a din that made Coney Island seem like a mausoleum. The folk dances were sandwiched in between social dancing and the pavilion was packed with youngsters. The loudspeaker blared full strength a nerve-gnawing medley of rock, twist, and some vague, mistreated relative of latin music. Around twelve-thirty tempers started to swell. Finally the dance group appeared. The idea of preserving regional dance is a laudable one and the government-sponsored Coros y Danzas has made some notable achievements, but this particular group was a sophisticated, uninspired, bored bunch of *señoritos* and *señoritas* just barely going through the motions, and what with the rudeness of the Fuengirola young, the infernal noise, the total absence of art, wit, or grace, we rose from our table, battered our way to the exit, and fled into the night. Nothing is more artificial than artificial folklore.

I wasn't the only one disgusted with the turn of events. Rafael Reyes stopped me in the street the next day and we went for a drink. The conversation led to the contest. Augustin "El Gitano," his wife's nephew, had won fifteen thousand pesetas and I figured Rafael would be pleased. When he said to me in a tone of mounting jaundice: "Pablo, it was badly organized," I was surprised and asked him why. He answered, "What kind of organizing pays off on a Sunday night in the form of a check with all the banks closed?" Augustin had left Monday morning, bright and early, his prize-money intact. The gypsies of Fuengirola were not too happy with their first flamenco contest.

My dream vision of a flamenco contest. A jury composed of *cabales* with at least one great old *cantaor* who can still sing. Unlimited funds and a big private salon. The prize-money substantial but not out of proportion since money makes even the best tremble and succumb. A private truck that runs continually to Jerez and back for fresh supplies of the best wines. The driver is given choice seats at the public finale. There are only guitarists who know how to and who love to accompany: no virtuosos permitted. Singers and guitarists are lodged in the finest hotel at the cost of the municipal government. Let's get down to basics: who is more important to the country—a flamenco artist or a tourist? Preliminaries last from two weeks to a year, depending on the number of contestants. Six or seven tape recorders are going all the time. No one is permitted who is not an *aficionado* or who does not passionately want to become one. On the first day there is a banquet: a real fraternal gathering between jury and singers. *Anyone who wants to sing can sing.* Jury will talk to singers. These are not candidates for the bar; they are singers. It's all right to ask them where they come from, when they began singing, who their favorite singers are. The singers can equally ask questions of the jury—might make for some funny surprises. The official preliminary sessions are held late at night since this is the proper time for the unfolding of the flamenco drama. At least two hours before each session, wine and *tapas* are laid out for all and there is a real tuning up: singer and guitarist get to know each other so there is a harmony for the moment of official singing; the singer has ample time in a cordial atmosphere to relax, thaw out his voice and his nerves, and is really predisposed to sing at the official hour.

A jury member in doubt may ask a singer to repeat. This is a good way of judging whether he is a mechanical performer or an authentic *cantaor*. The same device can be used to help those singers, unaccustomed to public singing, who in spite of the two-hour tune-up are still nervous. All the singers and the jury are together in one room. This is not a secretive, shameful gathering. *The contest is secondary.* First is the reality that men have come together to exchange creative feelings and knowledge. After each official session the jury will meet to exchange impressions. No one is afraid of being influenced. All are *cabales* and therefore willing to learn. Select *juergas* will take place during the length of the contest. It is in these extra-official sessions where the pure spontaneous essences of the world of flamenco exist and they will be taped also. But discreetly, in the background: the machine here is aiding man, not controlling him. Nobody will even notice if the machine breaks down. Biographies of the singers will be made and *coplas* will be compiled. Those singers who are eliminated will be given return tickets to their home towns and consolation prizes. Those who almost made the finals will get larger consolation prizes.

The winners will be chosen in private—that is, from elimination within the preliminary sessions. No competitive public ballyhoo finale. Afterwards, in order to present the singers to the public, a formal theatrical performance will be carefully arranged with elegance and dignity. There will be wine for the singers backstage. I will give a short, juicy speech on any one of the rich flamenco themes and I will introduce the singers. The performance will be studded by two unique dance numbers. One, the regional dance performed by those country people who still keep it alive in their traditional fiestas and not some tired, gum-chewing, government-sponsored student group on whom the regional costume looks absurd; two, the finest flamenco dancers, one male and one female, maybe "El Farruco" and Carmen Carrera, a young *sevillana* who just by raising her arms creates a silent *jonda ¡ay! The* tickets will be at popular prices so those among the people who care to see the best of their heritage can afford to do so. After the public performance there will be a private dinner for the winners, losers, and the organizers: a sort of *fin de fiesta* lasting into infinity: naturally, *anyone who wants to sing can sing.*

9

Yo nunca a mi ley falté
que te tengo tan presente
como la primera vez.

I never broke my word:
You're with me
Like the very first time.

North of Málaga, to Granada, there's a winding road that climbs the hills and for ten miles in the twists and turns you can still see the sea and the city below. I once made the trip before dawn; the sun rose in the hills and with the play of light on peak and slope, the long rolling landscape of olive and almond trees in the first light, the bakery we entered in Loja as they were removing the bread from the huge oven, our hunger fed on the hot round loaves and the smell of the bakery, the exuberance of the trip born in such a morning—I became drunk and sustained a wild humor that startled my companions who had only seen me taut and somber in my life in Fuengirola. If the same trip happened now I'd be singing my own unique imitation of *cante flamenco*.

We started early one December morning and as we climbed the Monte de Málaga, we stopped at several *ventas*, drank coffee and *anís* to warm our blood against the cool mountain air and to celebrate the day. We were Pepe Baena, his brother Paco, Ramón Moreno, the singer "El Niño de la Loma," and Pablo "El Americano." In a sudden move, sparked by Pepe Baena, we were going to Montefrío to see Manuel Ávila. The awareness that in a few hours I would be talking to him and hearing him sing spiced the liquor, my spirit, and the landscape that was moving away too quickly. We entered the plateau country and fifteen miles past Loja turned off the highway and headed straight north on a dirt road, slowly climbed into the sierra, wound around a mountain pass, and there was Montefrío below us and behind it the white gleaming mass of the Sierra Nevada.

It was midday when we reached the hill town. We stepped into a café on the main street, ordered wine, and asked for Manuel. He had gone into the country that morning to slaughter some goats. In ten minutes half the town including the policeman were searching for him. We had a few more wines and chatted with the townsmen. Though strongly *andaluz*, these *granadinos* and their town had a somber northern feeling. The houses were not lime-white nor was their humor salted with the southern *guasa*, the teasing thrust and riposte. They were hill people, silent and contained, and I sensed strong passions that might erupt savagely. The *malagueño* floods the day and night with speech, makes vocal banquets of his passion and his sensibility, and these people were laconic by comparison. But they were friendly enough to us. They knew that Manuel had won a prize in the Fuengirola contest, they were proud of him and impressed that *señoritos* from Málaga had traveled a hundred miles to see him. We waited for the singer until the hunger for food was too much and we went to the *fonda* to eat. In the middle of the meal in came Manuel Ávila.

Manuel appears before you as if what is enervating and destructive in the twentieth century has not yet reached him. If you see him standing there in a suit about twenty years out of fashion, his skull too large for his small body, that crazy blend of wildness and tenderness distilled in the sound of his voice—you know this man is of another time and place. And Montefrio *is* of another era. Tucked away in the northwest corner of the province, forty miles from Granada and eighty from Málaga, removed from highways, it lives from its olives, wheat, grains, goats, and sheep. Its dirt roads lead west to Córdoba, north to Jaen, and south to Málaga, and its muleteers, along with goods brought back the songs that were popular in each generation. But in the flamenco genre, the song that rises from the mountain streams and soars over this whole area is the *serrana*, with its wild, climbing repetitive tonality and this is one of the songs that Manuel Ávila sings best. He works his own small piece of land, has a small butcher shop in town, smokes hams and sausages in the attic and cellar of his house. The rest of the time he sings. Even his nervousness is a personal neurasthenia rather than the environmental anxiety of modern man. He has ignored the basic reality that society, the "other," is a potential threat to the individual, and so he is *loco*, which is his nickname in Montefrio. And if when he opens his mouth to sing and he sees laughter or teasing, he fumbles to put the sound back into his entrails, and that is a part of his awkwardness. But when he doesn't care about that "other," when passion or wine carry him downstream, his male flame, vulnerable yet enduring, wild but capable of caress, free from calculation, gives off a glow that seduces everyone. Sometimes the flame smokes and sputters, but one glimmer of sympathy is enough to get it blazing. And then they may call him any name.

He came into the *fonda* dishevelled, in work clothes, complaining that we should have let him know we were coming, but behind the complaint I saw the excitement that we had come to see him and that he would sing for us that night. Baena laughed: "We didn't come to see you. We came for the chickens you promised us." Manuel sat down and drank some wine with us. "Look," he said suddenly, "I'm going to change my clothes, find the guitarist, and meet you here later." He was too keyed up to stay and eat.

Manuel Ávila learned flamenco almost entirely from records. This means that he learned both the structure of a style and the manner of executing it by imitating records note for note and so his own creativity was restricted. His fullness and majesty of execution were also cut down because there just wasn't enough space on the old seventy-eights to include the complete classical "suite," which consisted of the preparatory song, the more difficult ascending one, and the *macho*, or dramatic ending. Having sung very little with a guitar, Manuel is bewildered by the tonal complications and the terrible range of guitar accompaniment, and it often takes him hours to find his proper tone. In his early years—he is now fifty-three—he toyed with the styles of the virtuoso singers, since they were so much in vogue, but the falsetto was an essential element of their technique and Manuel Ávila is not a man who can fake for any length of time. He copied them because they were popular, but slowly his temperament and his purity guided him towards the *jondo* styles and the *jondo* singers and so now he sings the versions of the great classic flamencos: "La Niña de los Peines," Tomás Pavón, Manuel Torres, Antonio Chacón, Pepe "El de la Matrona," Antonio Mairena. He has a fantastic ear and he makes you shiver with delight when he sings the *liviana* of Mairena and the *soleares* of Tomás Pavón.

Flamenco is a fusing of antagonistic essences: a cry to a fixed beat, a weeping "on time," a fragmenting of melody, a personal utterance within a traditional form. Sometimes, after a few hours of singing with people who are sympathetic, inflamed by the wine and the music, Manuel is able to reach for a moment that fullness in which technique and passion become one. Then, confident, he leaves the confining museum of the records. But he needs more practice, more singing with a guitar, more listening to good singers in intimate sessions so that he will no longer have to think about the formal problems. Then I wonder what his singing would be like. Not his sound. His sound is there and in the long run, since it is very rare for a singer to have everything—technique, creativity, emotional depth, *duende*—it is the sound that affects us.

Up until the last five years Manuel Ávila had rarely sung outside of Montefrio or Granada. Then he hurled himself, gaining confidence with each prize, into the contests of Jerez, Málaga, and Fuengirola. Apart from satisfying his hunger to sing and to hear good singing, apart from making him known to a handful of good *aficionados,* these contests have harmed him more than anything else. His purity as a man and as a singer was bizarre among the envy, mistrust, and greed that dominated, and being very vulnerable, he was often laughed at and suffered acutely. But more important, since his strangeness in the social world will exist until he goes into the grave, the contests muddied the purity of his *afición* by increasing his desire to be an *artista*—that is, to be not a butcher but rather a glamorous idol. The professionals teased him for being a hick and so his dreams turned to the desire to be the smooth, polished showman, smartly dressed with all the accessories that success brings. Moreover, the anti-flamenco norms practiced in the contests, especially the one of spot singing, cut a singer like Ávila down to one quarter of his capacity. The professionals and those who "remember" were able to slip by. But an authentic flamenco like Manuel, who doesn't know what he's going to sing beforehand, is confused by categories and by spot singing. After he won first prize in Málaga for the *serrana,* he had to perform along with the other winners in an official *fin de fiesta* spectacle. It was one of the most vulgar artificial settings for any kind of performance, let alone flamenco. A thousand people seated at tables, eating, drinking, and talking in a huge open-air pavilion, the stage a good seventy yards away. A master of ceremonies came out, introduced each singer, announced the prize he had won, and handed him his check. The singer, a puppet wound up by the money-key, promptly sang his song into a microphone and into the din of an audience that was not listening. On that stage Manuel Ávila was a eucalyptus tree in a hothouse. A few moments before, he asked me nervously: "Pablo, what should I sing?" "Sing the *soleares* of Tomás; you sing them so well." "Okay, that's what I'll do." The master of ceremonies introduced him, he gave his boxer's salute, hands clasped overhead, and started singing—*por siguiriyas!* In an atmosphere begging for smooth rehearsed singing he was himself: a pure flamenco. That's why I'm so drawn to Manuel Ávila. I see all of his shortcomings but for me he still is *el cante.* Surround him, nourish him with a true flamenco atmosphere and he will flower. Place him amid plastic and tinsel and he is disconcerted: the mask that is required slips off and awkwardness sets in. The only true atmosphere for Manuel Ávila is the closed-door session.

Juan Gambero Martin, "El Niño de la Loma," was born fifty-four years ago just a kilometer from the cottage where I am living. Neighbors have told me about coming back from town at night, hearing Martinillo sing, and standing there entranced at his prodigiously sweet voice. At the age of eighteen this voice, and the hope of making it pay, made him give up tending goats and pigs. He went into "folklore." It was the period of the Opera Flamenca and he traveled with one of the troupes, sang his *fandanguillo*, and suffered through the picaresque ups and downs of *el arte*. But he soon returned to his home town. The life of an artist was not for him because he is an introverted, serene, almost laconic, retiring man, ill-suited for the flourishes and the quick-change masks of the theatre. Although once in a while he made short sallies with a traveling troupe, he sang mostly in private fiestas. He worked at odd jobs, got married, and raised a family. From the end of the Civil War till about 1956 he earned very little from *cante*. During that period only the Opera Flamenca men were making money. Martin once told me that if he had money he would not sing. On seeing the surprised look on my face he added that of course he'd sing for friends in intimate *fiestas*. With the birth of the Costa del Sol, the flamenco renaissance, and the contests, Martin returned to the flamenco scene. He won prizes in Córdoba in 1958 and 1959, made a sweep of the large first prizes for the *malagueña* in both Málaga and Fuengirola in 1962, and returned the next year to win prizes in both places again. He made records, sang in the pavilions of the fairs, and rode the crest of flamenco popularity in his local area.

As a singer Martin is shaped by two opposing sources. One, the songs of Málaga taught to him by a stone-cutter from Coín, Frasquito Jiménez, who died a few years ago in his seventies, and two, the professional virtuosos of the Opera Flamenca—that is, classic flamenco and the frills of the modern school. And although he is aware of the enormous difference in value between the two he cannot rid himself of the prettifying influences of the latter. He is one of the strangest singers I've ever met. An imposing virile-looking man, tall, big, with a dark leonine head and straight black hair, you imagine he will make the sound of a lion. Instead, it is a cultivated, effective voice that is a fashionable suit covering his deeper being. And what that deeper being is we will never know because Martin keeps it carefully concealed. He relies on technical mastery, sure execution, superior physical resources, and he never abandons these controls. Except for one moment and this is in the style of the *taranta*, the song of the mines. Here, in the broken-toned melody of this song, Martin releases a delicate, plaintive feeling and a few piercing drops of a wilder lament. Perhaps Martin received some terrible blow to his manhood that made him forever lock the door to his vulnerability. I don't know, but I wonder what his singing would be like if he could open that door.

Ten years ago José Baena Romero was another Fuengirola mason looking for a day's pay. Today he is the head of a construction company that grosses millions of pesetas with a payroll of a hundred and fifty laborers. Always passionately interested in flamenco, he once studied the guitar and has built up an excellent record and tape collection. As an *aficionado* he has reached a certain point and goes no further because of prejudices in taste and because his business activities and a huge family leave him very little time to fully cultivate his *afición*. Although records are invaluable, the *aficionado* really learns through hearing singers in private sessions where the *cabal* is present. Baena's *afición* is enormous but he can't make the step from *aficionado* to *entendido* for many reasons. In order to be an *entendido* you have to be a remarkable human being. You have to be a lover of delicate sentiment and of raw harshness, of weeping lament and of ironic laughter, of wild, untamed mountain sound as well as the sound of urban back streets, of coastal melancholia and full-lunged, merry country shouting, of melody and aphonia, of heel-and-toe and hand-clapping percussion, and of fertile dramatic silence. Above all you have to be a lover of truth, capable of receiving and expressing feelings with an open heart and an open mind, an exposer of sham, be it of self or in others. All this plus a mastery of the vast labyrinth of historical and technical phenomena make an *entendido.* At the very top of this difficult order is the *cabal.* All *aficionados* struggle towards the goals of human fullness that are involved in *cante*; very few achieve them.

The sincerity of Baena as an *aficionado* and as a person is unquestionable. He is no vulgar *nouveau riche* but generous, straight, and with peasant roots that are fiercely alive. He has plenty of guts and I have seen him puncture phonies. But the too rapid leap from one economic and social class into another has upset his equilibrium. And since his personality, so ripe for change, has thrived on the moral, social, and psychological circumstances that come with the conversion of a small backward town to a prosperous modern resort, he carries this restlessness to the world of flamenco. He also suffers from the national illness, *patriotismo chico,* the fierce impulse to raise the banner of the local town or area higher than any other and at any cost. Baena organized the Fuengirola contests. He knew what true *afición* is, how and where it is nourished, yet swept along by the times, he attacked the contest as if he were planning the construction of a skyscraper. I come to flamenco after ten years of rudderless wandering in the dominion of art, a completely imitative frozen singer, unable to get down to my deeper self, and so I feed on those flamenco phenomena that liberate me for *my* song. And I try to resist certain basic currents of my historic moment. Is it any wonder there is a barrier between us? But in spite of the barrier, and this is the Spanish paradox, we seek each other out, we argue violently, we desperately try to convince one another, we yell and make terrible faces and we end up embracing each other.

> *Empiezo la primera*
> *en nombre de Dios*
> *perderé la vergüenza*
> *y alzaré la vóz.*

> I sing the first one
> In the name of God
> Then I'll lose my shame
> And I'll raise my voice.

At the entrance to Montefrío, when you drop steeply from the mountain pass and cross over the bridge, there is a bar called "Chacón." In the middle of the main room is a small iron stove

115

with a flue running straight up to the ceiling and the barboy keeps feeding it almond shells. The stove is small but throws off a lot of heat and the men who come in warm their hands. We sat down, ordered Montilla and waited for Manuel Ávila. The bar was quiet: the countrymen had not yet come in from the hills and the orchards for their Sunday-night drinking. Baena held forth on one of his favorite themes:

"That's the way to sing flamenco, like Manuel Vallejo, with melody, faithful to the rhythm. He was a nightingale singing."

"Pepe, Vallejo was a beautiful singer, but there are other ways to sing flamenco," said Ramón Moreno.

"Then it's no longer flamenco. It's gypsy and it doesn't have the value of the other."

"El Niño de la Loma" was silent. These discussions bored him. Nowadays everybody and his brother knew all about flamenco. Especially those who couldn't sing. I too was fed up with words and was dying to hear Manuel Ávila again. But whereas Martín coasted and endured, I consumed myself with impatience. And sometimes I think this is the strongest reason why flamenco is *andaluz*. Because of the ability of the *andaluz* to endure banalities and irritations with a tranquil stoicism. Which is a prime requisite for a *juerga*. It is physically exhausting to drink, get excited, angry, sad, loving for the five to ten hours a *juerga* may last, and the constant seesaw from sublime heights to insipid vulgarity is fatiguing. For me. The *andaluz* swims in emotional contrast like a fish. The bar filled up and became noisy. We went upstairs to a private room, ordered some more wine and hot *tapas*, and waited for Manuel. He finally showed up with the guitarist and a young gypsy.

Rafael Jiménez is a barber by trade and an *enamorado* of the guitar. He is self-taught, lacks maturity and execution, but makes up for it in feeling and a good sense of rhythm. He is a very serious boy, silent and reserved before strangers. He took out the guitar and began tuning it. Baena reached for it and strummed it a little. No one said anything about his playing. In almost every session there is a natural waiting period accompanied by a reluctance to begin, to be the first to break the silence. Every authentic singer knows that it takes a while to get warmed up and if there are

116

strangers present he is especially uneasy about singing cold. The flamenco says: "You have to break the voice." And that's exactly it. You have to sing a few songs, drink some more wine, become immersed in yourself and your songs, until you slowly cut away thinking about voice, technique, top-of-the-head memory, until the voice is "broken," thrown aside, and everything is fused to your deep flamenco sound. Until you forget about impressing anyone, pleasing them, or falling into ridicule, until you sing because at that moment it's what you have to do and you are alone: you are the singer with your song.

There are strong hierarchical patterns in Andalusia. In the bullfight the oldest matador kills the first bull but in *cante* the oldest or the best singer sings last. So the opening fell to the young gypsy, Melchor. He wore the boots, the hat, and the outward composure of a *tratante*, which he was, but he was nervous and imitated the devices of the modern gypsy idol, Porrinas de Badajoz. We all knew that it was too early in the session for an inexperienced singer like Melchor to reach even a moment of fullness, and we brought him along slowly, encouraging him. Then Martin sang the *malagueña* in that slightly nasal voice which is almost a non-flamenco sound but which still conveys the delicate sadness of the style. After thirty-five years his execution was perfect, the sound vaguely operatic and equilibrated. There was no question of breaking the voice. Martin began and ended on the same emotional pitch. Still, he never faked emotion, you never saw exaggerated facial expressions, hand-waving or chin-trembling. He served you the bird done to perfection but it lacked seasoning and the stuffing was flat.

Manuel Ávila sang from another flamenco continent. His sound is outdoor and tribal at the same time. From the very first note I felt his struggle to get his whole being into play. And since the *juerga* was warm and friendly he became mellow much more quickly than usual. His brother came in with a few friends and they sat down with us. There was no stopping Manuel. He sang, that night, *siguiriya, soleares, martinete, debla, malagueña, taranta, serrana, liviana, petenera, mirabrás, alegrías, bulerías, fandanguillo, curlugenera, cante de Juan Breva*. Baena and his brother, Ramón Moreno, and myself were contracting and swelling with each song. It was a personal anthology of *cante flamenco* and it was burning away pettiness, prejudice, pompousness, and everything that prevents men from opening their hearts to each other. Three different singers, a tireless guitar, endless wine: the atmosphere was one of mounting joy.

Around midnight the owner came in with a huge platter of fried chicken and a tray of bread: Manuel Ávila had kept his word. We all fell on the chicken and dipped the bread into the gravy. All of us except "El Loco." He didn't want to break the flow, his voice was hot and full, this was the only guitar he felt comfortable with, and he sang while we ate. The whole night he had to check himself to give the others a chance. He wasn't trying to best them, to compete, to make himself feel superior. It was just that this flow of song *had to come out.* And the most fervent *oles* crowned his singing. Martin, infected briefly by the fervor, came out of his dense apathy and poured a few honeyed drops of passion into a *cambio por siguiriyas.* He reached what was for him an unusual pitch, but still the struggle was mostly physical, and he quickly fell back into his usual repose. Melchor, now warm with the wine and the food, sang more freely and less imitatively, but the evening belonged to Manuel. The laughter, the teasing, the admiration, the passion, the constant chords of feeling, *the unifying us*—all converged in him. His tirelessness was incredible. It was as if each song were making him stronger rather than tiring him.

One of the townsmen, who had come in with Manuel's brother, a small, shabbily dressed middle-aged man, was by now high and bursting with pride. He sat between Baena and me.

"Some boy, our Manuel. You know they even wrote him up in the papers. Said that flamenco is still alive today because of Manuel. He's great, isn't he? You know what you ought to do? Put him in the theatre in Málaga. And make a lot of money."

Baena was feeling too good to be annoyed at this maudlin speech but it was three in the morning and he got up to announce our departure.

"Listen, we have to go. There's a hundred and fifty kilometers to drive and we have to go to work tomorrow."

"No, no. There's still a few songs I haven't sung yet. Why don't you wait till daylight? Then you can drive better. Come on, have some more wine."

"Listen, there's a hundred and fifty men go to work for me to-morrow and I have to be on the job. It's been great but we have to go."

Our mangily dressed friend got up and announced in a magistrate's tone: "All right, but you're not going until you have one last drink in my house." Baena looked at me as if to say: "Is this guy nuts? He looks like he needs a handout and here he's inviting all of us." We filed downstairs and Baena asked for the bill, which came to eight hundred pesetas. He took out a thousand-peseta note but Manuel Ávila stepped in: "No, no. Not here. You're in my town now and you don't pay."

Baena protested. It was a heavy bill for Manuel's modest income but he would not be moved and he paid the check. Baena started to give some money to Melchor but the gypsy shook his head: "I didn't come here to sing for money. I came with Manuel to sing for friends." Baena was surprised. I think it was the first time a gypsy had refused money from him and it shook him up.

It was very cold in the street. Coming from the warm bar, the wine, the food, and unused to cold, the *malagueños* shivered. We stopped in front of our host's house. It was an imposing two-story affair with a garden, beautiful wrought-iron gate and windows, and a big wooden door with brass studs and knocker. All twelve of us sank into a thick red carpet in the vestibule and entered a luxurious sitting-room with hand-carved silver bas-reliefs on the walls, plush chairs, elegant furniture with a big, long wooden table in the center of the room. Baena and I exchanged glances. Some handout. Our man went over to a liquor cabinet, pulled out a magnum of Carlos III cognac, and started to fill our glasses, saying: "You want vodka, you want gin, you want whiskey? Just tell me what you want." At this I burst out laughing and he joined in just because he was happy. The singing began again. A country boy who had been too afraid in the bar finally unloosened and sang the *serrana*. Melchor sang *alegrías*, Martín sang a beautiful *taranta*, and Manuel sang the *serrana* for which he had won the prize in Fuengirola. The singing lasted another good hour; our host burst with pleasure. Finally, at four in the morning, after a lot of protest, we got up and headed for the car. No one would have been able to drive if we'd stayed.

"Don't go Pablo. Spend a couple of days here in my house. . . . Pepe, wait for daylight. It's better for driving."

We stood there in the street in front of the car. We were no longer *malagueños, granadinos, señoritos,* workers, Spaniards, Americans. We were a family, brothers and cousins, who until tonight had been separated for a long time. We embraced each other in the street. Baena kissed Manuel and said that he would be back. As we got into the car and drove off, Manuel Ávila, open-throated, oblivious to the cold, was still singing.

10

El día del terremoto
llegó el aguita hasta arriba
pero no pudo llegar
adonde llegó mis fatigas.

The day of the earthquake
the water rose up
but it couldn't reach
where my sorrows reached.

*O*ver the past hundred and fifty years *cante flamenco* has been linked to the growth of the guitar. By playing one modern record you can hear the musical complications the flamenco guitar has reached. During the same period, however, the formal structure of the songs has remained more fixed, and so one of the great problems today is an equilibrated accompaniment wherein both singer and guitarist can express their personalities without once overpowering the other. In order to achieve this the guitarist must know and love the songs and the singer must be aware of tones and the basic guitar movements. The harmony must be sustained from the first guitar note that establishes the tonalities and the psychic essences of the song and prepares the entrance for the singer; it is carried through the pauses and silences where the guitar flows alone, rises into the dramatic ending, and returns to silence again. And all this must be accomplished to a fixed beat. A guitarist dragging or accelerating the rhythm over only a few notes destroys the dramatic unity. A singer losing the beat turns the song awkward. A guitarist making one extra flourish weakens the deep majesty of a *siguiriya* or a *soleá*. A singer starting in the wrong tone will shatter against the cliff of a terrible gamut and fall into ridicule. These and many other technical problems were made clear to me by José Núñez, Pepe "El de la Matrona," veteran professional singer who has dedicated sixty years to their solution. As I watched him, his lungs and figure straining in the extensions of the song, his left hand whipping or restraining the guitar, as I heard him roar "No!" to a singer and then proceed to show him the exact error by singing it, I sat in a silent stunned laughter and thought: this is what he calls "illustration." What emotional depths would he reach in the unbroken flow of wordless song?

How did I meet "El de la Matrona"? It was the winter of 1962 and I was broke. I had the basic necessities of life in the hills but I was unable to travel, hear new singers, and advance in my studies as much as I wanted to. With each experience I became aware of how much more there was to learn, and the lack of funds delayed my progress. In my last meeting with Anselmo González Climent in San Roque, we spent a beautiful night and morning in a local bar reading to each other our works in progress. He had started a series of essays on fifty singers and I marvelled at the fertility of his mind that spawned so many ideas on the flamenco theme. And with each work his language has become more lucid and more dense at the same time, just like an old singer whose sound is a fusion of the infinite phenomena of living—deep and subterranean but penetrating immediately. Anselmo encouraged me—he doesn't know the strength he gave me that day—and promised to write to a friend in Madrid to try and get me a grant. And so a few months later I went to Madrid to speak to this friend, Antonio

Amado, director of the Colegio Mayor de Guadalupe, a residence for South American students. I went there not as Paul Hecht but as that new personage formed through living four years among *andaluces* and three among flamencos. Formerly I had been deliberately "indifferent" about clothes, to show my scorn for the uniform of the times, but now I was dressing to fit my new definite, if hybrid, identity. And not only was I going "to town" but to Madrid, *La Corte,* so I put on my new tailor-made olive-green suit, the cloth sold to me by Rafael Reyes' sons (I found out later they had swindled me but I really didn't care: the color was beautiful). The tailor was a passionate admirer of Pepe Marchena, leader of the Opera Flamenca school, and he imitated perfectly the style of his idol. I hadn't dared to say a word of criticism against Marchena for fear the tailor would deliberately botch the suit and make me look like an idiot. I wore a dark shirt, tieless, which is the flamenco touch, had my pointy-toed shoes gleaming. I stepped into the academic decor of the Colegio de Guadalupe and coolly announced myself when the receptionist asked my name as Pablo "El Americano." She blinked. "Pardon me?" I repeated it and she announced it through the telephone to the director.

Antonio Amado received me with a great cordiality and a little smile on his face as if to say, "This is a case." We were soon deep in a long conversation about my life in the world of flamenco. He was an ardent *aficionado* but a very busy man, and he reluctantly pulled himself away from the "closed-door session" of our dialogue because by this time there was a long line of people in the waiting room. But not before he asked me to return to the Colegio in a few days and give a lecture on some flamenco theme. His mind was racing with plans for a combination lecture and *juerga;* he would invite the press and get Pepe "El de la Matrona" to attend. Antonio Amado was the first person, outside of Málaga, not only to accept the character of Pablo "El Americano," but to extend it into dimensions I hadn't even dreamed of. His imagination and enthusiasm swept me into a situation like one you might find in a Unamuno novel where the author steps in and threatens the protagonist with death. Well, here Pablo "El Americano" was, threatening to run away with Paul Hecht, because I had only previously "sung" in intimate sessions. Now I was asked to "sing" on a stage. Pablo

"El Americano" laughingly said "yes," but Paul Hecht was afraid. But the workings of this new identity had helped dissolve a timidity, a deliberate coarseness to hide that timidity, and a heavy dogmatic seriousness. In becoming Pablo "El Americano" I began to enjoy playing roles, but these were supported by the fact that I was saying what I really felt. And since this new identity needed the reaction of the other person to give it life, I was seeing that other more clearly: I was no longer running from him. The flamenco knows or intuits his witness. But he attempts to break through to him rather than flee.

I had two days to prepare the lecture. And then I thought, no, I'll translate sections from the first three chapters of my book. That would be better than any hastily prepared dissertation on some formal aspect of *cante*—I knew I was no *entendido*. I was primarily fascinated by the flamenco way of being up to the point where it had transformed my life and I would tell them a little bit of the story. It might be a warmer prologue for the singing. Before the lecture, we, a few friends, newspapermen, "El de la Matrona," were to have dinner at the Colegio. But first, there was an apéritif in the director's waiting room, a flamenco apéritif consisting of *vino fino* of Jerez and some *tapas*. Along with the excitement of reading my work was the one of meeting "El de la Matrona," whose sounds in the *serrana* and the *soleares de Triana* in the Hispavox Anthology are among the most impressive in flamenco. He came in, a small-boned old man with fierce eyes and a deep voice that was a sword—a magician's sword that flashed a mercurial humor and a thrusting certainty of self. Only the spoken film can capture the tones, the half-tones, of his vocal gestures kindled by the look in the eye, the hand movements, the wheeling of body and neck. He came in and the force and form of his personality made him the immediate center of attention that lasted until five in the morning, when he left.

The occupational disease of the *cantaor* is not deafness, or tuberculosis, or damage to the vocal chords, as many people think. Just as the *rumba*, the *guajira*, and the *colombiana* are made flamenco, so is hypochondria. There are hypochondria *grande* and *chico*, hypochondria with all the anguish of a *siguiriya*, and melodramatic hypochondria *por fandanguillos*. There is even hypochrondria *por chuflas*.[1] "El de la Matrona" had a terrible cold. His throat was impossibly sore and of course he would not be able to sing. Naturally he couldn't smoke or drink either. But what wine was that, Fino San Patricio? Well, in that case he'd have one *copita*: "It opened the appetite." About ten minutes later I saw him inhaling joyously on a big long Havana, his glass empty, and I went over to him to get it refilled. I couldn't get the glass out of his hand. "Pepe, it's to fill it." Without pausing in his dialogue he gave up the glass, and the evening began its artistic ascent.

We went in for dinner, about fifteen of us at one long table. The soup, the roast beef, the red wine, were spiced by Pepe's *golpes*:[2] luminous examples of *gracia sevillana*. Even his anecdotes are improvised: they never come out the same way. This is clearly analogous to *cante*. The authentic singer does not "remember": he creates according to what is inside and around him at the moment. That's why he never repeats the same song. During the meal, Dr. Jorge Ordóñez Sierra, who has written the most thorough classification of flamenco styles up to now, teasingly drew "El de la Matrona" out on several flamenco themes. The singer speaks intelligently on the subject because he limits himself to his personal experience, which is vast, and does not exaggerate or invent myths. At the same time, he has a strong pedagogical impulse; he loves to instruct, and although he roars like a lion and slashes the other person's ego, the latter must swallow this because "El de la Matrona" proceeds to correct by singing, that is, by making himself vulnerable in return. Too often, in the world of *cante*, many connoisseurs find fault but they do not follow it up with the best argument—actual singing. In one particular session the old lion was so harsh he literally destroyed the nerve and force of Manuel Ávila, who was having trouble finding his proper tone, and afterwards I said to him: "Pepe, I know it was for his own good, but why didn't you wait until he finished the song? It's not flamenco to cut in in the middle." He answered with the smile of a grand-

[1] *Chuflas* is a *cante chico* danced to the *tanguillo* or *por bulerías* and is mocking and teasing both in verse and in movement.

[2] *Golpe* is a spontaneous, improvised humor as opposed to the calculated joke, anecdote, or heavy tease.

father caught with his fingers in the cookie jar. "You're right, but if I'd waited I'd probably have forgotten." Manuel Ávila, although cursing and grumbling later, would sooner hear one solemn *bien* from the old bear than all the praise and endearments I could give him. Those who take Pepe's criticism grumble, curse, object, but they do it afterwards: in the heat of the moment they accept it because they respect his knowledge. The drama occurs because even the worst singer has a tremendous ego and reacts violently to even mild criticism let alone a fierce "No!" And that's why, in the sessions, watching "El de la Matrona" react is as exciting as the singing itself. The guitar makes its prelude, the singer begins and that face of Pepe's, mouth pursed in astonished rage, eyes wielding knife thrusts, is a powerful pantomime enacting both sermon and anathema. But when they sing well he acknowledges it also. The singer tempered in "El de la Matrona's" forge would be made of an unbreakable metal, because it could only be someone just as proud of his person and his art as the *maestro* and who would roar back at him—someone who would accept and revere the teaching but who would assert his own creativity.

This virile vitality that "El de la Matrona" spills out in a session is the same that has governed his life as a singer. Born in Triana (across the river from Seville) in 1887, he inherited the songs of the last third of the century, the richest in the known history of fla- menco. He left Seville at an early age, established himself in Madrid, and has lived there ever since. Although known to the inner circle of *aficionados*, he has spent many lean years as a singer, because the same fierce "No!" that he lets loose at a song badly sung was made at the changes brought in by the Opera Flamenca, the Ballet Flamenco, and the other commercializations of the modern era. Changes, which apart from affecting the styles themselves, toppled the *cantaor* from his patriarchal perch at the top of the flamenco hierarchy and placed him in a sad, secondary role as background for the dancer or as another number in a variety show. A Pepe "El de la Matrona," an Aurelio de Cádiz, startle us because their sound, their psychic and physical stance, bring us back to an era when majesty, dignity, a fierce pride in self, were natural conditions of the *cantaor*. And the way they sit in the chair, the way they wait, the way they listen to the opening chords, the way they tune up—are all tangible manifestations of this other-century stance. "El de la Matrona," save for a picaresque trip to America during the First World War, and a few tours, one with Vicente Escudero, has avoided the theatre and has sung mainly in private fiestas, carefully weighing his listeners and retaining the Caliph-like quality of the nineteenth-century singer. With the new wave of interest in flamenco he has made a few records, none of which he is satisfied with, and has given recitals in select places like the Sorbonne. All his life, since he has chosen to sing only to serious *aficionados* or to intellectuals, he has earned very little, but in return, he has retained his integrity and his art, and is now recognized as a pedestal, a source, a practicing authority.

The meal was over and with it my nervousness. The only other time I had spoken in public was in a poetry recital at Columbia University when I was twenty-two. The Spanish departments of the City Colleges of New York were holding a competition, and I was the pride and joy of Brooklyn College. I got up to recite a poem by Unamuno, my knees trembling and clanging, and I was saved by a little man with a face out of Velázquez and a suit a nameless shade of faded brown, who kept nodding and smiling to me and who pulled me through. But now, the sherry, the Valdepeñas, the cognac, the food, the laughter at the table, had all put me "at my tone." I was at the desired mellow state of the *cantaor* and I could have spoken at the White House or at the Pardo. We filed into the lecture hall where about a hundred and fifty people were waiting and I pulled "El de la Matrona" onto the speakers platform. He sat on my right, Antonio Amado on my left introduced me, and the show was on.

It was possibly the most unorthodox lecture given in that hall. In the first place, I translated directly, without preparation, from English to Spanish, having to pause at times to find the proper phrase and aware that the syntax and the grammar were often bizarre. But it didn't matter. The audience felt the drama of my attempt to reach them, no doubt heightened by the act of translation, and I in return felt their sympathy. Unconsciously, in my first public expression of my intense flamenco experiences, I was trying to do what Ortega y Gasset describes, in his book on Velázquez, as the ideal way of speaking in public:

> To speak as one should . . . is to achieve, little by little, the disintegration of the mass of audience and to make each listener remain alone, more alone than when he is alone in his house; to make each one become submerged in that radical solitude which is the authentic reality of his intransferable and personal life, in that dramatic and fertile solitude, in which each finds himself alone face to face with the problems of his own humanity, without anything getting in the way, face to face with the always frightening figure that is truth. To speak in public as one should is to antedate the apparent society in which men ordinarily believe they exist to the substantial authentic solitude that each one of them is: therefore, to decompose, to disperse the impersonal and unitary compact which is the public into a multitude of pure and trembling solitudes.[3]

On reading those fragments of the first three chapters that described the essential qualities of the singers and of those flamenco norms that made first impact on me, I was describing the realities of a way of being, the flamenco way of being. It was the terribly beautiful human way of enacting certain values that had caused a revolution in me. Because I had always been striving, in vain, to fully embrace those values: faithfulness to one's self, rejection of any kind of coercion of creative freedom, the courage to express the truth, the free non-calculating spending of one's vitality. It was the human immediacy of the flamenco expression that awakened me. I saw in the authentic singer a need to move the witness that did not conflict with the freedom of his singing. On the contrary: they were one. I saw that I had been singing for too long in an unpeopled wilderness of my brain. Now I wanted to sing about an amazing discovery—about the world, the world of things and people, of individuals and of society, the world of struggle and of song: the world of flamenco. And miracle of miracles, in telling fearlessly about this world I was telling more about myself than

[3] Translated by the author from José Ortega y Gasset, *Velázquez*, Revista de Occidente (Madrid, 1959), p. 85.

in those years when I was annotating what I thought were the unique convolutions of my brain and my sensibility. I thought then that I was making a new art but I was only a seismograph recording remote tremors. On the scene where the earthquake was taking place I said nothing. Now, on listening to a singer without voice, without lungs, reach the centers where nerves and heart are wounded or given ecstasy, the shape of my destiny was made clear. The flamenco sound projected with a terrible lucidity the only role that could give my life meaning: I had to speak directly to men, without fear, from the very center of the struggle, what I saw and felt. There was no problem. If I were an artist the speech would be song.

In that lecture hall my need to communicate directly was so strong that at one point I turned to "El de la Matrona," and said: "You understand me, Pepe?" That grave Solomon gave a slow approving nod to the excited novice and I continued. I spaced the reading with two of his recorded songs, ideal accompaniment since they made real, exciting sound and thus gave life to my word "sound." The audience was beautifully attentive. The reading ended; I was flying in euphoric space and several people, I can't remember who, came up to tell me how much they enjoyed it.

We left the lecture hall and the intellectual session for a more intimate salon and although in appearance we were a far cry from the classical *juerga*, suggesting rather some sophisticated soirée, a sense of flamenco time and behavior had already invaded us. We sat in a circle facing the patriarch, we drank the sacramental wine, we talked and joked, all the while steeped in expectancy. The singing was the one thing in everyone's mind but we approached it obliquely. And we waited. At last Pepe, really in a rosy mood for singing, fell into a trap baited by two young *aficionados* from Córdoba; feigning anger at their errors, he said he would "illustrate" what he meant; naturally with his throat a ruin, that was all he could do. The first note of illustration began at two A.M. and ended at five.

I was stunned. His records had not prepared me for the vital force of his performance. I remember sitting there shaking my head: I was out of breath *listening*. He carried the line into in-

129

credible extensions but it was never a vulgar display of physical resources tacked on as a virtuoso ending. It was always the proper length for the majestic emotion conveyed; from the very first note of *temple*, through the entrance, in each line with the rise of defiant struggle and the fall into an almost Hebraic weeping, there was a terrible exact harmony of rhythm and emotion between singer and guitarist. The force of "El de la Matrona's" singing lies in its totality, that is, in the perfect equilibrium of all the formal aspects linked to a subterranean sound of defiance and lament uttered by an unmistakable flamenco voice. Many *aficionados* claim that "El de la Matrona" does not have *duende*. García Lorca, in a fantastic essay, marvelously elaborated the theme of *duende*, but he far from exhausted it, especially within the infinite flamenco phenomena. Lorca says: "Angel and Muse approach from without; the Angel sheds light and the Muse gives form . . . but the *Duende* . . . must come to life in the nethermost recesses of the blood. The *Duende* . . . will not approach at all if he does not see the possibility of death."[4] Who knows. Maybe the *duende* will only approach after the artist has made his life-long struggle with the muse and with the angel, after his intelligence and his sensibility have struggled with the formal aspects of his art so that they are fused into his creative force, so that he does not have to remember them at the moment of creation and then the *duende* will come or not according to the anguished need of the creator to express, to communicate. For a long time the vision of *duende* in flamenco has been centered mainly in the *cante* of Manuel Torres. But everybody says he was an "insecure" singer. Does this mean that the "secure" singer cannot have *duende*? Pepe "El de la Matrona" has an ego which perpetually clamors for release; he also has a brain; he also has a fierce appetite for life which anyone who has ever been with him immediately perceives. He drinks more than anyone, he eats more, he talks more, and if he is happy with the company, he'll sing more than anyone else. But he is also eighty and he is Spanish. No one needs to give him a lecture about death. Every time he sings *por soleares* and *por siguiriyas*, as they should be sung, exposing his art and his physical strength, his vital force is challeng-

[4] From Federico García Lorca, *Poet in New York* (New York: Grove Press, 1955), pp. 156–162.

ing the disappearance of that force. And that is his sound. Maybe up to now he has frightened the *duende*. Maybe when he is a hundred and becomes a little tired, the *duende* will approach, accept the challenge, and then that weeping sound will be unbearable.

I sat in the elegant lounge and I listened to his songs. In my three intense years with flamenco I had not heard them before. Because whoever their creators were, and no one knows for sure, they are definitely of an era before the phonograph and they have not been recorded. "El de la Matrona," in the *jondo* styles—*por soleares, por siguiriyas, por tonás, por martinetes*—belongs to the school of Triana, less known and less widespread than those of other areas in Seville, of Jerez, and of Cádiz. In addition, he sings the *serrana*, and *caña*, the *malagueña*, the many styles of *levante*, the *petenera, tientos, alegrías, caracoles, mirabrás*, and I have even heard him in a *rumba flamenca* in which he beat out the rhythm with his fingers on a chair with a driving force that held us captive. All these styles, *grande* and *chico*, in the voice of "El de la Matrona" take on *jondo* nuances, some more, some less, but all are impregnated with that majestic stamp of his manner of being. Or as he says: "There is no *cante grande* or *cante chico*: it's the singer who makes a song *grande* or *chico*." The majestic creative force of José Núñez pervades every movement, vocal and physical. From the initial repose, the concentration hurled into the first *¡ay!* into the ensuing convolutions, he swings and wheels on the edge of the chair, his hands open and clench, his feet pound the bare skeleton of the beat, and he is water rushing through an irrigation ditch: streams run off to nourish green orchards or thirsty plots, tumble down terraces, and his voice is the central ditch rushing through the valley into the sea. It is the artist using every expressive organ at his command.

And then after three hours of singing something very interesting happened. On attempting the difficult songs of the forge, the *toná* and the *martinete*, his voice tired, he couldn't find the tone, and he used a false, higher pitched one. I hadn't noticed it but Elías Téres, *aficionado*, who had been accompanying him on the guitar, stepped in firmly and said, "No, Pepe, not like that." I thought the old lion would tear his head off. But he quietly accepted it. It seems like an insignificant detail but here was demonstrated precisely what makes a *cabal*: knowledge imparted in a firm human way that makes the singer strive for perfection. Because the authentic singer always struggles for greater depth when his witness demands it and Elías Téres knew that you can't find *lo jondo* with a false voice.

It is men like Elías Téres, like "El de la Matrona," Aurelio Sellés, Anselmo González Climent, José Luque, Pepe Navarro, José Blas Vega, who provoke in me the vision of an ideal flamenco academy dedicated to the conservation and the practice of this art. Provided that the flamencos do not kill each other off in the first week, such an academy would be more effective and more transcendent than any series of contests, at least, in the way these latter have been evolving the past few years. Having been in the middle of several of them I know the results are envy, hatred, injustice, ulcers: in short, a bad taste in the mouth. Singers are rejected; others are awarded prizes without anyone being told why. I don't see how this helps preserve *cante*. I don't see what is learned or gained except sums of money and the possibility of jobs in night clubs or in the modern *cafés cantante*. Because on the Costa del Sol, in Seville, and in Madrid, many of the working artists are former contest winners. And any *aficionado* knows that flamenco has no authentic life in a night club. But a self-supporting academy where song, guitar, and dance are governed and practiced by leading artists, *cabales*, and *aficionados* who are devoted to flamenco—such an organism would both conserve and create.

At first glance, the idea of a flamenco institution seems anti-flamenco and seems contrary to everything I have been saying in this book. Of course, the inner world of flamenco as a heritage passed down by one generation of *aficionados* to the next will survive, in its destined time, apart from any outside organized institution. I simply see a flamenco academy as nothing more than a *superior closed-door session* with important but secondary activities. Flamenco stays alive when its norms are kept, and it is in the closed-door session where they are kept most purely. When other activities—contests, recitals, lectures, studies—*replace* the session, the norms are forgotten. Historians, sociologists, writers, musicologists, may bring valuable information, but it is essential that they first saturate themselves in the true atmosphere. They must learn the songs, learn how to behave in a session, know how to ask for songs, know how to listen: they must *live* flamenco and then their ideas will have more substance. The academy would have, as invaluable aids, a library and a record and tape collection. But the session would be the live workshop where both the practicing and the theoretizing *aficionado* could advance in their art and their studies. And the measure of the academy's success would be that on any given evening, artists, teachers, pupils, and *aficionados* could get together spontaneously and have a superior session.

In such an academy I conceive of scholarships for both incipient singers and intellectuals. Committees would go regularly into the provinces—imagine the pleasure and excitement of covering Andalusia province by province in such trips—to seek out *aficionados*, young and old, encourage their *afición*, and bring the most outstanding to the academy. I think of how a Manuel Ávila and a hundred others like him would benefit by this. Thus the academy would have meaning in the present and not merely be a vehicle for an art of the past. It would be an organism preoccupied not with financial success but only in functioning independently and so would be able to preserve its integrity. No paying patron could demand his *fandanguillo* or dictate norms.

It would be difficult but not impossible to create this academy. We know who the best artists are in song, guitar, and dance: there are not so many of them. We know the writers and the *cabales* who have published important works and who have taken part in the most important flamenco acts: there are not so many of them. The money? The operating costs of rent and salaries for the teachers could easily be covered by select public recitals and an occasional international tour. The enacting of such a project need not be merely fantasy. It requires the energy of a few men who are passionately involved with flamenco not for gain but because they are simply *los de la afición*. A few men who really exist.

The session ended. It was five in the morning but I'm sure if someone had said: "Let's get some chicken in one of the *ventas*," "El de la Matrona" would have been the first to move. And after some food and wine, I'm sure he would have begun singing again. And this is another reason why those who criticize him respect him: they know he has *afición*. This word, used so often in the world of flamenco, can be applied to only a few. To those who are interested in flamenco because it nourishes their lives as a unique form of expression and for no other reason. That's why flamenco has always been a thing of minorities: of a small group of ardent individuals. Because after thirty or forty years on this earth, to remain an individual already indicates a unique struggle. The session ended but a friendship began with several men I met there that night. I had come to Madrid, a stranger, and immediately, without pomp, they had invited me into their lives. And I gave them the first fruit of what had been happening to me in the world of flamenco. This complete human directness and immediacy of treatment is a Spanish characteristic that enables you to endure the other immense frustrations of the social structure. But it is the essential nature of society, any society, to limit the soaring of the individual spirit. It's what we are asked to hand over when we become a part of it. So many Spaniards tell me: "Pablo, you don't know Spain. You only see the good things here." They tell me the same thing in the world of flamenco. But it's not true. I see the evil, I see the greed, the envy, the injustice, the hypocrisy. What they don't know is that here in Spain, through contact with a few unique individuals, my destiny, as a man and as an artist, after so many years of fleeing from it, finally takes root in the daily struggle, the daily cultivation, and this is what holds me here: my life and my struggle is joined to theirs and we give each other strength so as to be able to continue the struggle within our "radical solitude." And it is no coincidence that this has taken place in Spain. I see the evil. I see that their society does its best to wear them down, but I also see that they refuse to give up their individual flames: they keep on singing.

I walked through the streets of Madrid in the approaching dawn, pondering the eternal struggle between the individual and society, but my body and spirit were elated and suffused with the night's events. I had tasted a few distilled drops of a warming liquor from a unique artist, I had heard the *cante* of Pepe "El de la Matrona," and I had communicated a little bit of my own song.

11

En el campo nada importa
cantar bien o cantar mal
mas llegando donde hay gente
cantar bien o no cantar.

In the fields it doesn't matter
If you sing badly or well
But in front of people
Sing well or don't sing.

I returned to Málaga and landed in the middle of a Saturday-night session at the Peña. The singing was going on and I tried to hold in what had happened in Madrid but I couldn't. In a few minutes I blurted it all out and told them that the names of Diego, Manolillo, and Ángel were on the lips and in the minds of the Madrid *aficionados*. They took it very calmly. What impressed them most was that I had been with Pepe "El de la Matrona" and had heard him sing.

Up to then my role in the Peña had been a passive one. I was ingesting the experience and the knowledge they had to offer. But

now Pablo "El Americano" was feeling his oats. I argued, protested, rejected, proclaimed with the passion of any flamenco. And
I schemed and planned. I wanted to bring Manuel Ávila to Málaga.
The Peña needed the stimulus of new singers to offset the extra-
flamenco intrusions and to return to its primary function of singing
and listening to singing. I knew the experience would be of lasting
benefit for Manuel. It would give him much needed confidence
and at the same time he would learn the songs of Málaga from
Diego and Manolillo "El Herraor." The men of the Peña had heard
him in Fuengirola, had admired his sound and his *afición*, and they
agreed to pay for the trip and the night's lodgings in Málaga. So
I took off for Montefrío again: Sancho Panza in search of his Don
Quijote. Moving towards Manuel Ávila in the luxury of a Volks-
wagon bus, chauffeured by its owner, a young Canadian photog-
rapher, the landscape from the Granada road, seen and felt in late
afternoon and twilight, swept me into a wine-like exhilaration.
I only regretted that Manolillo or Diego was not with me. I had
already entered the phase of flamenco obsession that needed song
to crown and sustain exuberance.

It was already dark when we got to Montefrío. I found Manuel
in a bar. He was drinking with a friend who kept smiling at me
with his own variation of that smile I had come to know so well—
the one that patted me on the shoulder and said: "Isn't it great that
you speak Spanish, love flamenco and my Manuel, and here you
are in Montefrío and *what'll you have to drink?*" And in a little
while I was high. The steady filling of my glass with a white
Cordoban wine, which was a good thirty proof, charged my
exuberance. Which led to a flow of speech and an almost dangerous
moment when I really stuck my foot in it. Manuel introduced me
to a few men, the conversation led to *cante*, and they asked him
to sing. He hesitated, there was a lot of noise in the bar, and I
could see he wanted to go off to a private place. Still radiant from
my public-speaking success in Madrid, I told them the story of
when I asked Diego to sing and he said to me: "Quiet, stupid." I
explained to them how intimacy and spontaneity were so important
and how delicate were the circumstances in which singing unfolds.
My little lesson in the art of flamenco was not received well. One
chunky red-faced townsman angrily muttered: "We don't need

anybody to tell us how to act with our Manuel." Another youngish curly-haired *señorito* made it plain he resented being called stupid. It was a blind, absurd flare-up of misunderstanding. I saw the anger in their faces and in a crazy split second thought of Garcia Lorca who was killed in Granada. Manuel was very upset. I backed against the wall and tried to talk my way out of it. I explained that I wasn't calling anyone stupid, that the anecdote was to reflect on my own ignorance, and that if I wanted to call anyone stupid I would do it directly and not slyly. This last thrust broke through to them more effectively than all the defensive parrying. But although they realized I had not meant to offend, the cold fact remained that I, an outsider, had told them how to act, and that's what had cut them. As I walked around the town the next day, the same faces looked at me with a chiseled sullen hostility. My expansive wine-touched tongue had made what for them was a graceless stroke, and it stopped the potential movement towards a good session. I had forgotten I was an outsider.

We took off for Málaga the next day. Alone in the car, Manolo's hypochondria blossomed into a dizzying variety of exotic plants. He was nervous about going to Málaga, he couldn't shake off the stigma of the small-towner in the capital, and his fears multiplied into a huge sum of ailments. But this time I was ready for him and as we moved down from the sierra past Loja and down the winding Monte de Málaga to the sea, doctor and patient took irregular swallows of a bottled remedy that is always modern.

Manuel's blend of sensitivity and nervousness falls into an exact ordained fate in a country like Spain. I see him standing in a bar gesticulating and hurling his incoherent speech and he is a Prince Myshkin standing among muzhiks and petit-bourgeois. A Myshkin who has no formal education and who is the son of a farmer. The wild bard of a popular art practiced by an aristocratic minority. In every town in Spain there is a *loco* like Manuel Ávila. A *loco* who works at his craft during the day and who at night, in the café or tavern, cultivates and unleashes through speech or song his wounded sensitivity, his passionate reaction to the human scene. He is a *loco* because his capacity for fantasy, for feeling and expressing, is unique and it disturbs the onlooker. And when I wander through these towns the *locos* smell me out. They sense a blood brother who seems a touch cooler, a touch more cunning in that shaky truce men call society. A brother who seems less vulnerable. But they know. They know that the distance between us is scant and that some unknown series of defeats and illuminations could close the gap and I would enter that very potential shape of my destiny which is to be one of them. So they smell me out, they know me, just like the dogs in Fuengirola who have an unerring instinct for those foreigners in the cafés who will feed them scraps.

Manuel Ávila is a special kind of *loco* because he is beyond pathos. He needs others but clings to no one, and his aloneness is way out on some singular ledge of nerves and heart. The difference is that his defeats, his rat-in-a-trap scurrying, his absolute unfitness as a social man, all disappear when he makes his sound. They disappear for him and for the worker and intellectual, the artist and the businessman, the coward and the hero, the romantic and the cynic who cluster around that sound and are pierced by it. But when he's not singing he is lost, he forgets the triumphs because he lives only in the moment of now and he becomes a nervous hypochondriac. So his life is a diabolical seesaw and most of the time he is dangling desperately in space; he endures, but once in a while the seesaw tips and he comes down.

The two *locos*, the wild bard from the hills of Granada and the clever-tongued pilgrim from Brooklyn, moved towards Málaga and the gestation of Manuel's singing.

Málaga on Saturday evenings stirs with a particular kind of homey intimacy. Provided you're not lonely and have enough money for food, wine, and a bed to rest your after-fiesta frame. The crowds are smaller than the huge anonymous throngs of the metropolis, though larger than in the classical *paseo* of the small Andalusian town; the same faces and bodies appear and reappear in other streets and bars. Just large, prosperous, and modern enough for a few glittering reminders of the big city—the cafeteria, the night club, the elegant bar—Málaga lacks the racial variety and the diversity of pleasurable, opiate, or infernal diversions one finds in New York, London, or Paris. In the confines of provincial Málaga, paradise on a Saturday night is reduced to the caress and alchemy of wine, the tasty easing of hunger, the vocal sparring on favorite street corners, and for the initiated, for the inner circle of errant pilgrims, jolly monks, pompous bishops, silent cardinals, and consumed saints—the potential of *cante flamenco*.

This night the salty masculine premises of Casa Luna were imbued with the presence of Manuel Ávila. A lot of visiting singers have flavored and soured the sessions of the Peña but none was so warmly received as *El Loco de Montefrío*—not only for the richness of his singing, because there have been better singers, but for the transparency of a heart that shows no malice or envy or petulance. The world of flamenco is no garden of Eden. It is filled with men who unbridle more feelings than ideas and many of the feelings are petty and destructive. So when a man like Manuel Ávila sits among them and projects no tones of banal egoism, of patronizing superiority, or of dogmatic heaviness, but simply and wholly, by singing and listening, radiates a love for *cante*, he burns away one of the great barriers between Spaniards, which is the ever present plague of *patriotismo chico*, the compulsive fanatical love for one's town and province that limits and excludes the rest of the world and prevents any kind of growth. The foreigner fares better; being a foreigner he doesn't count: he isn't dangerous. All he has to do is show sympathy and friendliness and he is welcomed. But a *granadino* coming to sing in Málaga has to run the gauntlet of the national disease. Manuel Ávila, with his heart in his throat, his unsophisticated openness, his childlike behavior, was the exact opposite of a threat and so was unanimously brought into the fold.

After the initial hubbub, Manuel Ávila opened the singing with the *liviana* of Antonio Mairena, who is one of the most technically complete singers today and who has lengthened the song to fit his amazing physical faculties. In a definite sense all singers imitate from either records or other singers, although there is no one alive today who can directly imitate the songs of the great nineteenth-century masters. But since it is impossible to reproduce the exact sound, since all men vocalize differently, since all men express themselves differently, that imitation always bears a personal stamp. It is the degree of richness in that personal expression that distinguishes one singer from another, the measure that a singer can free himself from the formal structure of the song, without deforming it. The problem is delicate. When Manuel Ávila imitates Mairena or anyone else, it's not a razing of the walls but a momentary soaring over the rooftop or a digging under the foundations. Mairena and Ávila both have voices *de rajo*, but in a song like the *serrana*, which requires a savage sonority to keep it tense and dramatic, Mairena's *rajo* is converted, almost dissolved, into an esthetic sound, while Manolo's *rajo* remains elemental: it's the sound of a shepherd. Manuel Ávila, less of an "artist," with less consciousness, less knowledge, fewer tricks, less theatricality, gives the sensation of singing what he is. But in flamenco, what ultimately counts are the deep substrata, the psychic caves, the locked rooms that very few singers express or struggle to express. Neither Mairena nor Manuel Ávila does this. Mairena, because he knows too much and will not relinquish that knowledge at the crucial moment, and Manuel, perhaps because he knows too little and cannot free himself from thinking about the formal problems. And both because of their special fears. Of all the singers mentioned in this book, the only ones whose singing is nothing but a struggle to reach those depths are La Fernanda de Utrera, and once in a long while, Ángel Luiggi. And it was precisely Ángel, consumed and embittered by Manuel's stealing of the limelight, who was the one person that night to reject his singing. Most of it was a lacerated envy, a wounding of his ego, but the rest was the natural antagonism between the singer who is *aduendado*[1] and the *cantaor largo*, the one with condition and temperament for the long sonorous line; the former's complaint is that this kind of singer is cold. But whereas Ángel's bitterness eats away the more generous proportions of his art, La Fernanda goes straight to her struggle intact and whole. And she has chosen as her means of expression the *cante por soleares*, supreme test of the flamenco, while Ángel has

[1] The word *aduendado* is applied to a singer who constantly struggles to get and express the deeper recesses the *duende* inhabits. Often, he is a singer with poor or limited physical resources, and so a great deal of the drama comes from the combat of gasping lungs or damaged vocal chords trying to express melody, rhythm, and the exact dimensions of the line. Such a singer naturally despises a *cantaor largo* because his physical struggle is "easier." In all search for *duende*, however, the physical struggle means nothing unless it is complemented by the psychic one.

chosen the *fandanguillo*, which is formally and psychically smaller.

Manuel Ávila fascinates and attracts me for the terrible breadth of his potentialities, none as yet fully realized. Although he has sung a lot he has barely cultivated his art. His isolation in Montefrío has prevented contact with other singers in live sessions with a guitar. He cannot be categorized within any fixed flamenco denomination. Although he has the faculties of a *cantaor largo*, he also has the psychic pull towards one of the great *cantaores aduendados*, Manuel Torres. Actually the best parallel is with Tomás Pavón, brother of "La Niña de los Peines." Tomás is a *cantaor largo* with magnetic vibrations of *duende*, and Manuel Ávila also sings his songs with a rich fullness. There is no style that Manuel Ávila disdains or that he doesn't try to sing. He is equally at home in the fixed beat of the danceable styles and in the *ad libitum* forms like the *malagueña* and the *taranta*. This is unusual in *cante*, for most singers are attracted to and perform well only in one particular group. With Manuel Ávila, the factor that involves him in all these diverse styles is his unusual *afición*: his incredible appetite for *all* the flamenco sounds. With this as a pillar of his being, some of that rich potential would have to blossom if only he had the opportunity to dedicate himself entirely to *cante*. In moments like this I dream that the Ford Foundation has given me a million dollars to travel around the world and drop appropriate funds on "cases" like Manuel Ávila. I don't think it would hurt him.

If Ángel rejected Manuel's singing, the other men of the Peña more than made up for it. Pepe Luque shook his head in silent, rapt approval. Villodre nodded pontifically and beamed blessings; Manolillo "El Herraor" grinned and unloosed his salty repertory of "*si señor, eso es, así se canta, viva tu papá.*"[2] And the rest of the Peña followed suit. The guitarist, "Naranjito de Málaga," left early and Manuel, freed from thinking about the accompanying instrument, flowed into an unchecked outpour. He sang and he listened. He listened to Diego intone, with that antique thread of voice, a series of delicate *malagueñas* and his face in reaction was

[2] *Si senor*, literally "yes sir," is praise one notch above *eso es*, which means "that's it," the singer is on the right path.

that of an aged child signaling candid joy and tough approval at the same time. He laughed when he listened to Manolillo's unique versions of the *tango de El Piyayo*. He sat as tribal brother to Villodre's rusty-voiced renditions of the *siguiriya* and the *soleares* of Manuel Torres. Only with Ángel did the listening darken as the air was filled with bitter, competitive arrows. For a moment they sang to best each other but Ángel, wounded and limping, had to remain in the shadows. Manuel Ávila triumphed because his expression covered the majesty of diverse *jondo* styles, whereas Ángel, although swelling the style to its utmost, was imprisoned in the narrow backstreets of the *fandanguillo*. And Manuel triumphed because he had not come to compete. He listened because he loved, he listened to learn new things, he restlessly hungered to be penetrated and to penetrate all the flamenco forms that moved him. He was in his element, absorbing from the atmosphere the components that were life-sustaining: the good sounds, the sympathetic and admiring reactions, the general warmth and excitement. The *malagueños* balked and muttered that he still had a lot to learn, especially about the songs of Málaga, but much later I heard them praising and defending his *cante*. Pepe Luque got up and in the name of the Peña presented him with a box of cigars. This was the laurel wreath, the dazzling trophy of acceptance and success. Manuel Ávila held it in his hands, and joyfully responded—by singing. The session moved into its final stage of intensity with Manuel pouring for one and all the mellow wine of his song.

The Peña was both catalyst and medium for a social hunger within me that had been anesthetized through years of silence, exile, impotence, and flight. It *was* society, with all the dramatic tensions between possibility and reality that existed in that larger one and within each man, but it was small enough to function on an intimate human basis and thus allow me to maintain a balance, however irregular, between revolt and immersion. The writer writes alone at his desk, but only in the measure that he has lived with other men can his art have rich reverberations. In my early formative years I had used the solitude of the artist as an arrogant pose, a protective mask and armor to weather the agony and the confusion in the struggle between self and society. But such solitude was sterile. I had created almost nothing, and worse, I had retreated from humanity. In the turn of events, inner and outer, that led to my life in the Peña, in being a member of a group that came together to sing and to listen to singing, those social seeds that had been in the warehouse too long and which were on the point of rotting, finally were brought out into the light, were planted and cultivated in a fertile soil. By *social* I mean a clear, breathing, beyond-the-surface facing of the "other," or any and all "others." As a result my solitude in the hills of Mijas became a sonorous one.

The night that Manuel Ávila sang in the Peña we both made our successful "debut" in society. Perhaps only for a night, perhaps for longer, he as singer and I as intellectual organizer revitalized and restored the structure of the session to its essential form: a meeting and elaboration of *afición* where singing took first place. Not a few of the members became aware, through the full, sustained flamenco flow of the night, of the terrible deficiency in the previous months when non-flamenco activities predominated.

As the evening ended and we all wound our separate ways through the streets of Málaga, the Manolo of Montefrio and the Manolillo of Málaga walked arm in arm, nodding and smiling and singing to each other. They were oblivious to the theoreticians, the administrators, the politicians, and I watched them walk away. It was no accident they left together. They are the living substance of *cante*. All the rest is incidental.

12

*Los lamentos de un cautivo
no pueden llegar a España,
porque está la mar por medio
y se a hogan en el agua.*

The sorrows of a captive
Can never reach Spain,
Since the sea is in between
They drown in the water.

I can't sing flamenco. Though my heritage is
Ashkenazi, I weave the fantasy that some errant ancestor was a
Sephardic cantor, from Seville perhaps, and through him I inherit
a sound which is more synagogal than flamenco, but which contains some fragments and echoes of melodies and vocal ornaments
that are *andaluz.* I can't break my voice or pull the sound inside.
I can't make the weeping *jipío.* But once in a while, when the inner
climate is right, when the need to sing is strong enough, the sound
that comes out, apart from its comic exterior of impossible *melange,*
carries some sediment of feeling that is a deeper touch and not
just a tepid handshake.

Singing is a strange thing. How wonderfully we sing when we are alone. We think that both technique and passion fuse into a marvelous plant that yields both flower and fruit at the same time. But the moment we start to sing before people, the wind of self-consciousness shakes the plant, dries the leaves, and timid fragments float erratically down to earth. We sing in the bathtub out of exuberance; we sing romantically as some better Frank Sinatra; we sing the catchy tune of the moment, the tune that's in fashion; we sing the exotic songs of Latin America to widen the acts and play-acts of our limited repertory; we sing folk songs or work songs or political songs because they have special meaning for us, maybe their sounds have more guts; we sing the songs of our youth out of nostalgia or maybe in defiance of the new generation that makes a sound not ours. But to sing flamenco involves other dimensions. Dimensions of search into areas that involve risk and vulnerability. And in trying to sing it, not only did I discover some of the problems the *cantaor* works with, but also why so few singers are able to move the listener.

Normal social intercourse is an uneasy truce and it's hard to bring out feelings in a direct form that preserves the feelings in their purity and integrity. We are afraid and embarrassed for ourselves and for the "other" and so we coat our feelings, clean them up, sweeten, prettify, freeze them—we falsify them. What fascinated me in the world of flamenco, from the very beginning, was that as a standard of performance and reaction, false expression was not accepted. The delicate firm flame of an acute sensitivity to pseudo acts burned into me my own history of self-deceit. I had been a martyr without saintliness. At twenty-three, I entered a marriage that lasted four shaky years and finally flopped through a combination of adolescence and cowardice. My own. Afterwards, I took out the years of masochistic suffering on quite a few women.

An intellectual ashamed of his intelligence. With the laborer, the academician, the bourgeois, and the pseudo-bohemian I assumed a tough anti-intellectual pose in speech and gesture. I played Stanley Kowalski without Brando's tenderness and tried to bury that part of me that was the passionate student.

A writer who didn't write. Out of an inordinate desire to be loved by one and all I sealed up the defeats and the sorrows and

every once in a long while wrote a careful, cerebral lyric of exalta-
tion and praise pointed towards any other world but this one. About
this one I wrote nothing. The poems were proof of my superiority
over the herd. They were involved in sham but not me the poet.
With people, I was hard and critical; in verse, I wrote words exalt-
ing "humanity."

A rebel without courage. A revolutionary without a program. An
anarchist without convictions: not even was some *new* world to
be built from the ashes of this one. Over a period of ten years my
talent for pretense built a flourishing graveyard of pain and hatred
deep in my guts. In Fuengirola, the failures continued—with
women, with writing, with the people around me. I was turning
bitter. I had to unearth and confront my history of fraud or I was
headed for a "sickness unto death." The only way a writer faces
his own fraud is to write about it.

The working precepts of *cante* were not the cause of this con-
frontation with myself. They just speeded things up. And the
great thing was that revelation occurred not in a solemn, heavy,
puritanical atmosphere but amid laughter, teasing, wine, and song.
I fell into a garden of Eden that included all kinds of devils, satyrs,
and fauns—men who had taken all kinds of beatings and who
had emerged with an irony and a toughness and a tenderness you
heard in their songs.

After four and a half years in Andalusia I returned to New York.
The landscape changed from the olive, the fig, the almond, the
hot Mediterranean sun, the view to the sea, the planted terraces,
to brick and stone apartment houses, asphalt and concrete, the
skyscraper, TV antennae, endless stores and office buildings. From
the ox and the goat to the car and the truck. From the solitary
farmer on a country path to the seething humanity of the metropolis. From the rhythm of: "We'll see what the body says tomorrow"
to "Hurry up, it's late." Instead of eating under a rosebay canopy,
the pink flowers and green stems a cool shield from the sun, I
now ate in front of a talking picture box. Instead of going to the
Peña Juan Breva I went to the movies. Instead of with Manolillo
"El Herraor," I sat with my real father who was suffering under

the grind of driving a cab in the New York chaos. Instead of Pablo "El Americano" I was the anonymous Paul Hecht. I was lost once again. But I was now Paul Hecht *plus* Pablo "El Americano." My roots were in Bensonhurst, Jewish residential section in Brooklyn; its playgrounds and schoolyards had been my woods and battle-grounds, but the flowers of my manhood had blossomed in the hills of Mijas and the rhythms behind this blossoming were still in me. For a while, in odd moments of joy or whatever it is that one needs to express in some form of howl, cry, song, word, look—even in the New York insanity I made sounds that echoed the inner contours of Andalusia.

Seventy-two-year-old Mair José Benardete is a legendary figure at Brooklyn College who has dedicated his life to the teaching of Spanish literature. His face is a composite of Dostoevsky, Baude-laire, El Greco, and Ortega y Gasset. I mean he looks like them, comports and expresses himself as I imagine they did. He has prodded, irritated, trampled, inspired, encouraged students for forty years. But his major contribution is that he has made them think. The seeds of my involvement with Spain were sown when I was a student of Benardete's. He made literature a living thing and I carried his ideas, methods, gestures, and their total stimulus not only into other classrooms, but into other worlds I was to enter. When I came back from Spain I looked him up. He was very ex-cited about my pilgrimage in the world of flamenco; he praised and encouraged my work. I lectured to one of his classes. He gave me a needed lift when I was floundering, depressed and lost in New York, and he introduced me to some young poets, figures who emerged from the maelstrom of assassinations, murders, racial riots, the stench and gamut of violence, like some long lost rela-tives with whom I could sustain a vital dialogue and a friendship. This tells who he is more than pages of details: the seventy-two-year-old teacher was the link between the new generation of poets and an exile ten years older. He invited us to the college to attend a Christmas party.

The maestro, strict disciplinarian when it comes to study and scholarship, has always known how to break the absurd monotony of academic rhythms, how to defy the dehumanizing structures of formal education. One of the ways he did this was through his annual Christmas party which always had an Hispanic flavor even in the middle of Flatbush. There was always liquor and there was always song. Fifteen years earlier, returning from Mexico, I sang Mexican *rancheras* at one of his parties at nine in the morning and staggered around the college from class to class joyous just to be drunk in a place where it was forbidden. But that was just a green prologue to my formal debut as a singer of *cante flamenco*.

Benardete and his pupils sang a few Castilian Christmas songs, we sipped liqueur and then in his inimitable style, he announced: "And now, ladies and gentlemen, Paul Hecht will sing the real *cante jondo*." I looked at him as if to say: "Are you crazy? You just don't start singing flamenco like that without preparation, without wine, without some kind of warm-up, without someone *else* starting first." He completely ignored my look. Benardete knew nothing about the mechanics of *cante* but he knew, intuitively, that it was my moment to sing in public. He knew that after all the years of dispersion and silence, I was ready. And he was right. I stalled a little, nervously, quickly drank a few shots of rum and began to sing. I don't remember what or how. There was a pause. Some talk, more Christmas songs, more rum. Then the maestro signaled me to sing again. He sensed I was a little riper and had gotten over my initial fear. There must have been some thirty students in the room. It was a party and there was a lot of talking. I waited for silence. They kept on talking. I shouted, part petulant, part play-acting, part serious: "Silence! I won't sing with people talking." My exclamation was absurd and right at the same time.

Absurd because I wasn't really a *cantaor*, but right as an authentic flamenco gesture. If I was going to try to sing flamenco then I had to, consciously and unconsciously, immerse myself in its norms and rhythms. Because in order to communicate feeling publicly, which is what flamenco is, there is a risk of failure and rejection. It is not ordinary singing: there is no adornment to cling to if the inner expression is not coming through. And therefore it requires its own special atmosphere. I sang, maybe with more feeling, maybe not. There was no flamenco in the room to correct or spur me on. I was singing to strangers, to poet friends, to olive trees alive in my memory, to my teacher, and—for the joy of singing.

The romantic sees a landscape, a man, a woman, a social event, and from a rapid perception of surface and gesture, proceeds to elaborate an emotional ballet that takes off from the initial impulse, and he gets drunk on his own excitement or bliss. But he does not come to grips with that "other," does not immerse himself in it: he doesn't have a *relation* with it. He doesn't expose himself to the danger of receiving from or giving to it. Narcissus takes over and what was outside becomes incidental. Until my years in Andalusia, most of my actions and reactions were made within this kind of vision. The flamencos forced me to perceive a fuller one: the romantic vision is inadequate in an authentic flamenco session. The problem is linked to the phenomenon of time. No matter how sharp our intuition and perception, vital relations cannot be sustained *on the run*. Especially on the run away from the person or thing that has captured our attention. It's not a question of mere quantity of time spent but of genuine *involvement* in time. Nor is selection barred. On the contrary, we get involved with someone who attracts us. Either for their elegance, grace, wit, fantasy, their struggle, or their sickness. But in the world of flamenco one doesn't *make*, *kill*, or *check* time. One doesn't even spend time, but rather spends one's self in a time ordained by the situation. This idea is stressed throughout this book because it's an essential point of contrast between my life as an American and as a flamenco. Ed Botts, one of the young poets I met through Benardete, illuminated the whole thing for me. Six months after the event he told me: "You know what I remember most in meeting you? The first time I came to see you, you opened the door and said, 'Come in, come in,' *as if you had all the time in the world*." This behavior, so significant to Ed Botts, American, is a matter of course to the *andaluz* and the flamenco. There is always time in his world. For example: one day I went to Málaga to leave a message for Manolillo "El Herraor." He was working in the big wheat silo on the Málaga docks. The director of the silo and two other men working there are also members of the Peña. The silo is government run and is a huge enterprise, but walking in was like entering the house of an affectionate relative who hadn't seen you in a long time. Greetings, embraces, smiles, teasing, and before I knew it we were in the director's office shooting the breeze and sipping sherry *as if we had all the time in the world.* And we did.

Which leads to the second point of contrast that lacerated me on my return to New York. I sat in rabbi's offices, university waiting rooms, government buildings, relatives' homes, bars, restaurants, coffee shops, jazz clubs, parks, and movie houses. I stood on street corners, in supermarkets, bookshops, gallery openings, in the subway, in bus terminals, at parties. As a social investigator in Harlem I interviewed Negroes and Puerto Ricans who were applying for welfare. I watched and was dragged into the seething scene. I saw the dehumanization of mankind, the disappearance of the *person,* in full swing. And the people I met, curious about my life in Spain, said to me: "Do you mind if I ask you a *personal* question?" And then proceeded to ask me why I lived in Spain or what it was like. Let me answer all of you now. I don't mind. Within my irony and my protest I'm begging you to ask me a personal question. Make any kind of move towards me that will kindle a personal gesture, a personal smile, a personal howl, a personal word. Ask me a hundred million personal questions. I'm ready to bare my soul before strangers or friends. I'm not saving it. To your personal question I'll give you a personal answer. And in the rest of the time that's left to me, while I'm running around living, getting and consuming, giving and meditating, dreaming and acting—I'm going to make a *personal* sound: I'm going to make *my* sound. Not the wife's or the mother's and father's sound, not the President's or the television's, not the Madison Avenue or the Village sound, not *your* sound. Maybe at first it'll come out like a croak or a whisper, a whimper or a rusty chirp, but later on, when I get the hang of it, maybe there'll be a little more art in it and maybe not. But I'll enjoy it and maybe *one* listener will too.

And so I wandered through the sweating, freezing, hungry, surfeited multitudes of Brooklyn and Manhattan, more lonely than in the hills of Mijas; I walked around the neighborhood of my youth and childhood in Bensonhurst; I stood on Brooklyn Bridge and looked at the city. That year I was a foreigner in New York— that year of the murder of Kennedy, of the summer of the Harlem riots, the murder of Schwerner and so many others in the South, the organic eruptions of violence held so long in abeyance. I saw the increasing hold of mass media, the fantastic swirl of power and acquisition in the land of plenty, the transformation of man into a passive spectator in some compulsive trance-like stupor, I saw the hope of America only in its creative misfits. I was a foreigner. But I was no longer a foreigner in the world, in worlds, tiny and immense, where the human being still counted. And in Harlem, to and from work, in the subway, in Central Park, in public urinals, on any empty street—I sang flamenco. I sang to myself, to sympathetic listeners, and, in drunken moments, to people who weren't interested. Like some Good Humor man gone mad on a sweltering New York summer day giving away his ice cream, I sang my own special brand of tutti-frutti flamenco.

I put down the last pages of this book on a farm outside of Mijas, an old mill converted by Rogoway, the American painter who owns it, into a solid, lovely house surrounded by green growing plants and flowers. I'm back among the olive, the carob, the fig, the almond, the grapevine; back among the sound of running water, the burro's tragicomic bray, the goat's they're-slaughtering-me lament, the wind, the crickets, cicadas, and birds, the sound of some countryman guiding mule or horse through the sierra. I'm back among the sounds and sights of Andalusia. And through the window I see the neighbor, Antonio Porras, his aging wife and seven-year-old boy. They're planting corn. He's turning over the earth behind a team of oxen and she's dropping the kernels in the furrows. They finish up the task in the moonlight. Once again, my writing coincides with the neighbor's plowing and planting. And now I can answer a letter I just received from a friend in New York. She asks: "Are you singing? You were bursting to sing here." Yes, Jeriann, I'm singing. Here goes a song for you.

> *Vente tú a la vera mía*
> *que tenga una vez mi cuerpo*
> *un ratito de alegría.*
>
> Come over here to me
> So that my body can have
> A little bit of joy.

But wait, something else happened. I put down what I thought was the end of the book. It was Saturday, I felt good, and I went down to Málaga to celebrate. I hadn't been to a session in two months and I was ready: the first wine tasted good in my own song of preparation in my favorite bars. The Peña was packed and I found a seat in the corner between the guitarist and a young singer from Jaen. The singing began, the guitar melodiously mixed wine and sound, into a savoury herb and a hundred thoughts and sensations passed through my mind. I felt that all the words I had written were incidental, that only sitting there listening to the music, clapping hands, responding to the singer's effort, only being in the center of the live drama was what counted. Being there in the middle of the envy, the tenderness, the nervous egos, the vocal impulse, the separating distances, the brief moments of harmony and union. But something else was happening. The years of participation, of study, of submersion, of growing with and in this particular world had cut away the compulsive pose: I was no longer self-conscious and *I belonged there in that little room.* I had slipped in quietly without the usual fanfare, just like any other member, and I was sitting in the smaller of the two rooms among the minor leaguers and the newcomers. I wasn't Pablo "El Americano," flamencologist. I was just Pablo, just another *aficionado* drinking wine and listening to the singing.

The atmosphere was cold. Maybe they had heard the same singers too often, they were involved in problems concerning their roles in the August fair, at any rate, the session never got off the ground. The meeting broke up and we hit the street. There was a local fair that night in the district of Percheles, ancient workers' quarter the other side of the Guadalmedina River, and somebody said, "Let's go." For the first time, I didn't hesitate; I didn't go with my favorites or with the intellectuals to talk about *cante*: I just felt like drinking and hearing songs. We stopped a horse carriage and off we went singing. We were Pepe Navarro; Pepe Flújar, a mason in his fifties with a good hoarse flamenco voice and a rough, sweet disposition; Fernando Montoro, a twenty-seven-year-old chemistry instructor; a young Cordoban engineer; and me. Fernando Montoro and Pepe Navarro were used to singing in public. Flújar, the Cordoban, and I were not as good and much more timid. But that night we were all equally swept away with the need to sing, we plucked songs from everywhere, not able to wait for the others to finish so that we could get our own song out, but waiting and in good taste, within the same generic style, either crowning the other's song or preparing someone else's. There was no condescension, no one impressing or being superior. There was just an incredible delight in weaving the rich textures of a music we all loved. All those times I had sung alone in the streets of New York, working the few songs I knew over and over again, and now they came out in their proper terrain. I let out with a *martinete* of Manolo Caracol, faltered, and then finished it. Pepe Navarro pulled my hair and looked at me, surprised, as if to say: "You rascal, you've been practicing behind my back." I stood there beaming at him: his look was a prize.

The fair was small, made up of booths with food and wine and a few carnival rides. We drifted from booth to booth, drinking, oblivious to the carnival noise but not to each other. Pepe Navarro was in his element. The oldest and most learned, he sang variations of many different styles. But added to his own joy of expression was the one of an older man in harmonious union with generations much younger. Fernando Montoro, passionate student, followed Navarro in all the styles except the *malagueña*, in which Navarro is the master. But they sang to each other as equals.

We were five good *aficionados* re-living the story and the rhythms of flamenco in an open-air *feria* atmosphere, one of its natural locales. But the key to the night is that we *all* sang. We all took part. An old beggar, hat in hand, with a great smile, came up to us. He sang a *malagueña* with a raggedy charm. Then he started another song and Pepe Navarro cut in: "No man, that's not it." The beggar sweetly told him: "Okay, you sing it." After Navarro finished it, the old man said: "You're right, that's the way it is. I got confused." For a while he became part of the group. At four in the morning the wine began to hit us and we got a carriage back to the center of town. Navarro couldn't let us go without one more song. He traced a last delicate *malagueña* in that broken flute of a voice. We all stood in a circle, heads bumping together. Five men, sweetly drunk on a street corner, and singing. Best session I've ever been in. Until the next one.

Appendices

CANTE,
Definition and Classification

*A*ny classification or absolute definition of *cante* is bound to be arbitrary. I use here a philosophical approach to three major categories with the awareness that the *cantaor* is the ultimate determining factor. That is, the songs, in no matter what category they are placed, will vary according to the depth or the superficiality of the singer. Then again, within the generic styles themselves, there is great variation—as, for example, in a series, the songs of preparation, the songs defining the emotional and esthetic direction, and the songs crowning the series. Anselmo González Climent's *Flamencologia*[1] defines three major categories, as established by the flamencos, which I present here.

The classification I offer is by no means exhaustive and is purely

[1] (Madrid: Imprenta Sánchez Leal, 1955); 2nd ed. (Madrid: Escelicer, 1964).

personal. I have left out many styles rarely sung—many tending to fall into the category of folk song and almost the whole gamut of South American songs that have been incorporated into the flamenco genre.[2]

1. *Cante jondo.* Those styles in which the voice communicates in direct and virile tones the anguish of man facing "limit" situations, such as death, God, nature, solitude, and love, in the drama of existence. *Cante jondo* is the ultimate form of flamenco expression, consuming a man's entire integrity. It calls up the seriousness and concentration of the witness, the intimacy of closed doors, of half-shut eyes, of half-voice, for the desired atmosphere that surges up, encloses, and limits the *jondo* itself, as expressed in the following *siguiriya*:

> *Tan solamente a la tierra*
> *le cuento lo que me pasa*
> *porque en el mundo no encuentro*
> *persona de mi confianza.*

> Only to the earth
> Can I tell what is happening to me
> Because in this world I can't find
> One person to trust.

Cante jondo sung without guitar includes:

> *tonás*
> *martinetes*
> *carceleras*
> *deblas*
> *saetas.*

Cante jondo sung with guitar includes:

> *siguiriyas*
> *soleares*[3]
> *cañas.*

2. *Cante grande.* A reconciliation with that tragic destiny expressed in *cante jondo*, through either stoic resig-

[2] For a more complete classification, see the essay by Jorge Ordóñez Sierra, *Classificación del cante*, in Anselmo González Climent's book, *Cante en Córdoba* (Madrid: Escelicer, 1957).

[3] The rich gamut of the style *por soleares* eludes the definition offered here. Some *soleares* would fit into the category of *cante jondo*, and others into *cante grande*, as classified here.

nation or heroic impulse. Essences of intimate feelings, serious or delicate, are communicated through a vocalizing that strives to transcend the verse in an esthetic ordering of the voice. The participating witness in *cante jondo* is in *cante grande* an *aficionado* with free entrance and exit, in psychic balance, mixing tears with laughter, and orienting himself to the rich, expressive surface as well as to the profundity felt. The following *serrana* is a typical vehicle for such expression:

> Yo crié en mi rebaño
> a una cordera,
> de tanto acariciarla
> se volvió fiera.
> Que las mujeres
> de tanto acariciarlas
> fieras se vuelven.

> I raised in my flock
> A white lamb
> From caressing it too much
> It turned savage.
> And women,
> From caressing them too much
> Turn savage.

Cante grande includes:

> malagueñas
> livianas
> serranas
> polos
> peteneras
> tientos
> alboreás
> cantes de levante (including *tarantas*,
>   *cartageneras*, *tarantos*, *muricianas* and
>   *mineras*)
> granadinas and media granadina
> fandangos (including *camperos locales* of
>   Córdoba, Granada, and Málaga)
> jaberas
> rondeñas

> *caleseras*
> *temporeras*
> *trilleras.*

3. *Cante chico.* Placing the graver problems of humanity to one side, *cante chico* surprises and charms the listener through *gracia* and tends towards movement, dance, gesticulation— the theatrical. The relation of singer to witness is one of play and lightness; diversion is the goal, as in this *tango de Cádiz*:

> *Con el ¡ay, caray, caray!*
> *Mire usté qué fiestas*
> *va a haber en Caí [Cádiz].*
> *Luego qué hambre*
> *se va a pasar.*
> *¡Ay, caray, caray, cará!*

> With the *ay, caray, caray*
> What fiestas
> There are going to be in Cádiz!
> And later, what hunger
> They'll go through.
> *Ay, caray, caray, cará!*

Cante chico includes:

> *alegrías*
> *cantiñas*
> *romeras*
> *caracoles*
> *mirabrás*
> *tangos de Cádiz*
> *bulerías*
> *fandangos de Huelva*
> *fandanguillos*
> *sevillanas*
> *villancicos*
> *zambras*
> *tanguillos*
> *chuflas*
> *jaleos*
> *farruca*
> *garrotín*
> *guajiras.*

THE COPLA FLAMENCA

Del polvo de la tierra
saco yo coplas,
no bien se acaba una
ya tengo otra.

From the dust of the earth
I bring up poems,
As soon as one is over
I've got another one.

*O*ne of the wonders of *cante jondo*, apart from
its essential melody, consists in its poems. . . . The most infinite
gradations of pain and sorrow, set to the service of the most pure
and exact expression, beat in the triplets and quartets of the
siguiriya and its derivations. There is nothing its equal in all of
Spain, neither in stylization, nor in atmosphere or emotional pre-
cision. The metaphors that people our Andalusian songbook are
almost always within their orbit; there is no disproportion among
the spiritual members of the verse, and they take possession of the
heart in a definite manner. It is strange and wondrous how the

anonymous poet of the people extracts in three or four lines all the rare complexity of the highest sentimental moments in the life of man. There are *coplas* in which the lyrical tremor reaches a point only a few, numbered poets can attain.[1]

The poems, or *coplas*, of *cante flamenco* were born in the feelings, minds, and throats of particular singers and have come down to us orally. We don't know the names of the original composers but we do know the names of the singers who kept the poems alive through their song. Some *coplas* are adaptations of cultured poetry and a few were written by poets specifically for the flamenco genre. Only those that have the syntax, the phonetics, the conceptual aroma—in short, the authentic speech of the *andaluz*—have survived the test of time. They are the ones forged from the spirit, the ingenuity, the humor, the suffering, the erotic, social, and metaphysical attitudes of the people.

The most common *copla* is an octosyllabic quartet with loose alternate rime. Many are composed of three, five, and six lines of varying syllabic length. The singer often repeats and lengthens lines, depending on the traditional vocal ornaments of a given style. Poetic influences have been traced to the Mozarabic *jarchya*, the *romance*, or epic ballad, the Castilian and Manchegan *seguidillas*, and the *jota* of Aragon. Today, except on rare occasions, the singer no longer improvises new poems.[2] From the thousands in the anonymous songbook, he chooses the ones of his favorite singer, those common to a given musical style. But his choice of *coplas* is very personal. They fit his temperament and his vision and they reveal to us who he is.

Except for jailhouse songs and those of the forge, which tell of the persecutions, the trials and tribulations of the gypsy, the *coplas* are not anecdotal. They are lyrical and dramatic exclamations and confessions, pathetic or fierce sparks that inflame the imagination and make us see episodes and stories. But they themselves do not narrate. Spain is a country where the autobiography

[1] Federico García Lorca, *Obras Completas* (Madrid: Aguilar, 1960), p. 1520. Translated by the author.

[2] An interesting exception is the young singer, Pepe Meneses. Some of his *coplas* are composed for him by a friend, Paco Moreno, and they deal with Meneses' personal life. The few that I have heard are very good.

and the memoir have never flourished as literary genres. But the *coplas* are a tremendous trembling confessional.

Though the themes in the flamenco songbook are vast, the majority of the *coplas* deal with some form of love. The love of a man for a woman as companion, wife, mother, virgin, and *hembra*—the female in an animal sense. The variety and nuances of erotic expression are immense: delicate tenderness, the direct curse or threat, raw sensualism, platonic idealism, sententious irony, the pathetic plea, the flame of hate, picaresque humor, and once in a while the rending cry of the woman protesting her condition. Entangled in the love poems are the motifs of pain and sorrow. As in the melodies of the songs a wounded lyricism comes through.

The rest of the *coplas* are divided mostly between metaphysical, religious, and social attitudes. They abound in comments on poverty, injustice, the lack of Christian compassion in organized society, the frailties and deviltries of the human condition. And, of course, the *coplas* resound with the great theme of all Spanish art: death.

Many of the metaphors are taken from nature. The *andaluz* lives within a perpetual dialogue with the elements and so a tree is food, shelter, teacher, fuel, a quivering target for his emotions, as well as a plastic image.

I offer the reader a hundred *coplas* that move me. Depending on the individual poem, the translations are literal, slightly recreated, colloquial, and formal. The poems stand by themselves. With the singer and the guitar, the reverberation is even richer.

Qué equivocaíto vivía	How wrong was I living:
que quería un acaloramiento	I wanted heat
donde había una nevería.	Where there was only an ice house.

A mí se me da muy poco	I don't give a hoot
que el pájaro en la lamea	If the bird in the park
se múe de un árbol a otro.	Moves from one tree to another.

A mi puerta has de llamar	You will knock at my door
no te he de salir a abrir	I shall not come out to open
y me has de sentir llorar.	And you will feel me weeping.

163

The Wind Cried

Anda y no presumas más:
si te has de tirar al pozo,
¿pa qué miras al brocal?

Come on, don't be so uppity:
If you're gonna jump in the well
Why keep looking at the edge?

Te lo juro por mi mare,
que si tú caes malita
te doy caldo de mis carnes.

I swear it by my mother:
If you fall sick
I'll make you broth from my
    flesh.

Dices que no me puedes ver:
la cara te amarillea
de la fuerza del querer.

You say you despise me:
Yet your face turns yellow
From the force of love.

Yo me voy a volver loco,
porque una viña que tengo
la está vendimiando otro.

I'm going crazy:
Because a vineyard I have,
Someone else is picking it.

¿Para qué tanto llover?
Los ojitos tengo secos
de sembrar y no coger.

Why so much rain?
My eyes are dry
From sowing and never reaping.

Chiquilla, tú eres muy loca:
eres como las campanas,
que toíto el mundo las toca.

Girl, you're crazy;
You're like the bells:
Everyone rings them.

¿Qué tienen sus ojos
que cuando me miran,
los huesesitos, mare, de mi
    cuerpo
todos me los lastiman?

What can her eyes have;
When she looks at me,
Mother, the bones of my body
All hurt me.

A servir al rey me voy,
y el viento que da en tu puerta
son los suspiros que doy.

I go to serve the king:
The winds that touch your door
Are my sighs.

Cuando paso por tu puerta,
te rezo un Ave María,
como si estuvieras muerta.

When I pass by your door
I sing an Ave Maria
As if you were dead.

Esa mujer está sembrá:
va derramando mosquetas
por dondequiera que va.

That woman is planted:
She pours forth musk roses
Wherever she goes.

Tu querer y mi querer
aunque lo rieguen con llanto
no pueden prevalecer.

Your love and mine
Though watered with tears
Cannot last.

Diez años después de muerto
y de gusanos comío
letreros tendrán mis huesos
diciendo que te he querío.

Ten years dead
And eaten by worms
My bones will make signs
Saying that I loved you.

De pena me estoy muriendo
al ver que en el mundo vives
y ya para mí te has muerto.

I am dying of sorrow
To see that you live in the world
But are dead towards me.

Tu mare no dice ná:
tu mare es de las que muerden
con la boquita cerrá.

Your mother doesn't say a
    thing:
Your mother is one of those
    who bite
With their mouths closed.

Dices que soy mal gachó
siendo yo más gitanillo
que las costillas de Dios.

You say I'm a bad Andalusian
While I'm more gypsy
Than the ribs of God.

Yo no sé lo que me pasa
cuando me acuesto contigo
y me pides para la plaza.

I don't know what comes over
    me
When we go to bed
And you ask for money for
    market.

El limón con la canela
rebujaíto con el jazmín
así me huelen tus carnes
cuando tú te arrimas a mí.

Lemon and cinnamon
Blended with jasmine,
That's how your flesh smells
When you come close to me.

Cuando yo me muera
te pido encargo
que con las trenzas de tu
    pelo negro
me amarren las manos.

When I die
I entrust you
With the braids of your black
    hair
To tie my hands.

Si el querer que puse en ti
lo hubiera puesto en un perro,
se viniera detrás de mí.

If the love I gave to you
I'd have given to a dog
He would follow behind me.

The Wind Cried

La verdá, me da coraje:
que la quiera o no la quiera
eso, ¿qué le importa a naide?

Really it gets me mad:
That I love her or not,
Whose business is it?

Le dijo el tiempo al querer:
esa soberbia que tienes
yo te la castigaré.

Time said to Love:
That pride that you have
I'll punish you for it.

Tengo el gusto tan colmao
cuando te tengo a mi vera
si Dios me diera la muerte
yo quizá no la sintiera.

My pleasure is so full
When you're at my side
If God sent me death
I might not even feel it.

¿Dónde me arrimaré yo,
si no hay un pecho en el mundo
que quiere darme calor?

Where can I seek shelter
If there 's not one breast in the
    world
That will give me warmth?

Tengo yo un pozo en mi casa
y yo me muero de sed
porque la soga no alcanza.

I have a well in my house
And I'm dying of thirst
Because the rope does not reach.

¡Válgame los cielos!
¡Válgame la tierra!
¡Lo que acarrea un testigo falso
y una mala lengua!

My God in heaven
And on earth!
What power a false witness
And an evil tongue can have!

Ya se me murió mi mare;
una camisa que tengo
no encuentro quién me la lave.

My mother has died;
I can't find anyone
To wash the one shirt I have.

Que te den los cuatro vientos
porque no tienes ley
ni a la camisa del cuerpo.

Let the four winds beat on you
Because you've no respect
For even the shirt on your back.

Subí a la muralla
me respondió el viento:
¿Para qué tantos suspiritos
si ya no hay remedio?

I climbed the ramparts
The wind answered me:
Why so many sighs
When there's no more remedy?

Tengo yo un cañaverá,
mientras más cañas le corto,
más me quean que cortar.

Aunque en una cruz te pongas
vestío de Nazareno
y pegues las tres caídas,
en tus palabras no creo.

Déjalos que digan, digan,
y de mí formen historias;
que el que se muere queriendo
se va derechito a la gloria.

Aquel que tuvo la culpa,
mare, de mi perdición,
a cachitos se le caigan
las alas del corazón.

Me puse a ahondar un pozo
con mucho gusto y placer;
me salió amarguita el agua
le eché tierra y lo cegué.

Suerte negra, suerte perra
la suerte de la mujer,
que lo que el alma le pide
se lo prohibe el deber.

Anda vete, corre vete
que ya se me fué el amor;
quien se ha comío la yema
que se coma el cascarón.

Decirme a mí que te olvide
es predicar en desierto
machacar en hierro frío
y platicar con los muertos.

I have a reed field:
The more reeds I cut
The more are left to cut.

Though you put yourself on a
    cross
Dressed as the Nazarene
And take the three falls,
I will not believe your words.

Let them keep talking
And make up stories about me,
He who dies loving
Goes straight to glory.

He who was to blame,
Mother, for my perdition,
Let the wings of his heart
Fall away piece by piece.

I went to deepen a well
With joy and pleasure:
The water came up bitter
I threw in earth and closed it up.

Black luck, bitchy luck
The luck of a woman:
What the soul wants
Duty forbids.

Go on, get away
Love has left me.
He who has eaten the yolk
Let him eat the shell.

To tell me to forget you
Is to preach in the desert
Forge on cold steel
And talk with the dead.

The Wind Cried

Anda vete con la otra,	All right go with her
supuesto que la has querío	Since you love her,
que yo sembraré en mi huerto	And I'll plant in my orchard
la semilla del olvío.	The seed of oblivion.
Alcarraza de tu casa	Clay jar in your house,
Chiquilla, quisiera ser	Girl, I would like to be
para besarte los labios	So I could kiss your lips
cuando fueras a beber.	When you go to drink.
Soy desgraciaíto	I am unlucky
hasta pa'l andar,	Even in walking;
que los pasitos que yo doy	For the steps I take forward
p'alante	Turn back on me.
se vuelven p'atrás.	
Más mata una mala lengua	An evil tongue kills more
que las manos del verdugo;	Than the hands of the
que el verdugo mata a un	executioner;
hombre,	The executioner kills one,
una mala lengua a muchos.	An evil tongue many.
Permita Dios que te veas	I pray God you find yourself
sin chaqueta y sin calzones	Without clothing
en una higuera chumba	In a cactus
espantando gorriones.	Frightening sparrows.
Arbolito te secastes	Little tree you dried up
teniendo el aguita al pie,	Having water at your feet
en el tronco la firmeza	Firmness in your trunk
y en la ramita el querer.	And love in your branch.
Dice mi compañera	My companion says
que no la quiero:	I don't love her:
cuando la miro, la miro a la cara	When I look at her, I look at
y el sentío pierdo.	her face
	And lose my senses.
Si mi corazón tuviera	If my heart
vidrieras de cristal	Had little glass windows
te asomaras y lo vieras	You could look in and see
gotas de sangre llorar.	It weeping drops of blood.

168

Se murió la mare mía;
¡Ya no hay en el mundo mares,
Mare, la que yo tenía!

My mother has died;
There are no mothers in the
    world,
Mother, the one I had.

Es tu querer como el viento
y el mío como la piedra
que no tiene movimiento.

Your love is like the wind
And mine is like the stone:
It has no movement.

Te tengo comparaíta
con las piedras de la calle,
que las pisa toíto el mundo
y no se quejan a naide.[1]

I have you compared
With the stones in the street:
Everyone steps on them
And they complain to no one.

Cuando se muere algun pobre
qué solito va el entierro
y cuando se muere un rico
va la música y el clero.

When a poor man dies
How lonely is the funeral;
And when a rich man dies
There's music and clergy.

Hombre pobre huele a muerto,
a la hoyanca con él;
que el que no tiene pesetas
Requiescant in pace, amén.

A poor man smells of death
Into the hole with him,
For he who has no money
"Rest in peace," amen.

El aguita que se derrama
nadie la puede recoger,
ni el humo que va por el aire,
no el crédito de una mujer.

Water that is spilled
No one can gather
Nor smoke in the air
Nor a woman's honor.

Naide diga en este mundo
de este agua no beberé;
por muy turbia que la vea
le puede apretar la sed.

Let no one in this world say:
I won't drink this water;
As muddy as it seems
He may be driven by thirst.

Hasta la leña en el monte
tiene su separación·
una sirve para santos
y otra para hacer carbón.

Even the wood in the hills
Has its differences:
Some is used to make saints
And other to make charcoal.

[1] *Pisar* also means to mate (with birds).

The Wind Cried

Arbolito del campo
riega el rocío,
como yo riego las piedras de
    tu calle
con llanto mío.

Dew waters
The little tree in the field
As I water the stones of your
    street
With my weeping.

Yo no sé por dónde
ni por dónde no
se me ha liao esta soguita al
    cuello
sin saberlo yo.

I don't know where
I just don't know how
This rope got round my neck
Without my knowing it.

Tú eres la palma y yo el dátil
tú eres zarza, yo me enredo;
tú eres la rosa fragante
del jardín de mi recreo.

You are the palm and I the date
You are bramble, I'm entangled:
You are the fragrant rose
In the garden of my delight.

La tierra con ser la tierra
se comerá mi dolor;
al pie del almendro estuve
y no le corté la flor.

The earth being earth
It will consume my pain:
I was at the foot of the almond
    tree
And did not pluck the flower.

Dices que duermes sola
mientes como hay Dios
porque de noche con el
    pensamiento
dormimos los dos.

You say you sleep alone
By God you lie:
Because at night with thoughts
    of each other
We both sleep.

No sé por qué
la paloma aburre el nido
y no puede entrar en el.

I don't know why
The dove is vexed with the nest
And can't come in.

Er queré quita er sentío:
lo igo por esperensia,
porque a mí ma suseío.

Love takes away reason:
I say it from experience
Because it happened to me.

Yo me hago la ilusión,
luego me como de rabia
los puños del camisón.

I pretend it's so:
Then in rage I eat
The cuffs of my shirt.

Yo le pido a Dios
que tú me mires con los mismos
    ojitos
que te miro yo.

I ask God
For you to look at me the same
    way
I look at you.

Como tanto la quería
yo me la llevaíto por la
    carretera
le eché el sombrero a la cara
pa que l'aire no la diera.

I loved her so much
When I took her away along the
    highway
I tipped my hat over her face
So the wind wouldn't strike her.

Yo no sé por dónde
al espejito donde me miraba
se le fué el azogue.

I just don't know where
From the mirror I used to
    look at
The quicksilver went.

Quisiera ser como el aire
pa yo tenerte a mi vera
sin que lo notara naide.

I want to be like the air:
To have you at my side
Without anyone knowing it.

Dejé la puerta entorná
por si alguna vez te diera
la tentación de empujar.

I left the door ajar
In case sometime you might
Be tempted to push.

Si la lengua te se seca
con aire de perlesía,
no le eches la culpa a naide,
que son maldiciones mías.

If your tongue dries up
As if you were stricken with
    palsy
Don't blame anyone:
My curses did it.

Como gallinita muerta
que rueda en los muladares
te tienes que ver, serrana,
sin que te camele naide.

Like a dead hen
That rolls in the dungheap
That's the way you'll end up,
    girl,
Without anyone to love you.

A mi mujé en la lengua
le mordió un perro rabioso,
en seguía busqu'al perro
y lo harté de biscochos.

A mad dog bit my wife
On the tongue;
I ran out to find it
And stuffed it with biscuits.

The Wind Cried

Merecía esta serrana	This girl deserves
que la fundieran de nuevo	To be forged all over again
como funden las campanas.	Like they forge the bells.

Como tortolita	Like a turtledove
te fuí yo buscando,	I went looking for you,
Compañerita, de olivo en olivo,	Companion, from olive to olive
de ramito en ramo.	From branch to branch.

Yo no sé qué tiene	I don't know what
la yerbabuena de tu huertecito	The mint of your garden has
que tan bien me huele.	It smells so good.

En un cuartito los dos	The two of us in a room:
veneno que tú me dieras	Poison that you would give me
veneno tomara yo.	Poison I'd take.

El aire lloró	The wind cried
al ver las duquitas tan grandes	On seeing the terrible sorrows
de mi corazón.	Of my heart.

Cuando a tí te apartaron	When they took you
de la vera mía	From my side
a mí me daban tacitas de caldo	They gave me cups of broth:
y no las quería.	I refused them.

Tengo yo mis propias carnes	My very flesh has turned
del color de cera virgen	The color of virgin wax
que me ha puesta esta flamenca	This woman has got me so
que no me conoce naide.	Even my friends don't know me.

Yo he visto a un hombre vivir	I've seen a man live
con más de cien puñaladas	With more than a hundred knife
y luego le vi morir	wounds,
con una sola mirada.	And then I saw him die
	From a single glance.

Una ramita de azahar:	A branch of orange blossom:
qué poquita cosa es	What a little thing it is
pero cuántas naranjas da.	But how many oranges it gives.

Acaban de dar las doce	It just struck twelve
en el reló de la Audiencia:	On the courthouse clock:
entre jueces y escribanos	Between judges and scribes
me han leído la sentencia.	They've read me my sentence.
No me dolió la sentencia;	The sentence didn't pain me:
lo que a mí me dolió	What hurt
fué que ella estaba en la	Was that she was in court.
Audiencia.	
Todos le piden a Dios	Everyone asks God
la salud y la libertad	For health and freedom
y yo le pido la muerte	And I ask him for death:
que no me la quiere dar.	He won't give it to me.
Desgraciaíto aquel que come	Wretched is he who eats
el pan por manita ajena	Bread from another's hand;
siempre mirando a la cara	Always looking to see
si la ponen mala o buena.	If the face turns bad or kind.
Yo no soy el que era	I'm not the man I was
ni quien debía de ser	Nor the one I should be
soy un marco de tristeza	I'm a frame of sadness
pegaíto a la pared.	Stuck to the wall.
Doblaron las campanas,	The bells rang
creyeron que era la reina	They thought it was the queen
y era una pobre gitana.	And it was only a gypsy girl.
En tu corazoncito	You gave me a room
me diste un cuarto	In your heart
y no pude barrerlo	I couldn't keep it clean
por tanto trasto.	For all the trappings in it.
Yo no lo quiero	I don't want it
a menos que no quites	Unless you remove
trastos de en medio.	The junk between us.
Los ojos de la viuda	The eyes of the widow
van diciendo por la calle:	Are saying in the street
esta habitación se alquila	This room is for rent
porque no la habita naide.	Because no one lives here.

173

The Wind Cried

El día que tú naciste
el sol se vistió de limpio
y hubo en el cielo una juerga
que bailó hasta Jesucristo.

En la tienda del barbero
¿sabe usted lo que se dice?
Que el Señor le da pañuelos
al que no tiene narices.

Los pasitos que yo doy
qué murmuraítos son
otros tropiesan y caen
y no los murmuro yo.

El que no tiene parné
con el viento es comparao
que todos le huyen el bulto
por temor de un resfriao.

Si tu cara fuera iglesia
y tu cuarto fuera altar
y tu cama sepultura
vivo me fuera a enterrar.

Yo te lo tengo jurao:
dondequiera que te encuentre
tienes el entierro pagao.

Si mi mare no me casa
antes del domingo que viene
le pego fuego a la casa
con toíto lo que tiene.

Todavía guardo en mi cama
el hoyito que ella dejó
las cintitas de su pelo
y el peine que la peinó.

The day you were born
The sun got all dressed up
And there was a ball in heaven
That even Jesus danced at.

In the barber shop
You know what they're saying?
God gives handkerchiefs
To men without noses.

The moves that I make
Are mouthed by everyone;
Others trip and fall
I don't say a word.

He who has no money
Is compared with the wind:
Everyone ducks and flees him
For fear they'll catch a cold.

If your face were a church
And your room an altar
And your bed a grave
I'd go to be buried alive.

This is sworn and sealed:
Wherever I meet you
Your funeral is paid for.

If my mother doesn't get me
married
Before next Sunday,
I'm burning the house down
With everything in it.

I still keep in my bed
The imprint that she made
The ribbons from her hair
And the comb that she used.

Candela hice en el monte	I made a fire in the hills
vino el viento y la barrió;	The wind came and blew it out;
donde candelita hubo	Where there was fire
siempre cenizas quedó.	Ashes always remain.
Pa los pobres que nacen	For the poor who were born
pa desgraciaos,	To be unlucky
hasta los mismos juncos	Even the river rush
son jorobaos.	Is twisted.
Toítas las mañanas	Every day
me levanto y digo:	I wake up and say:
El lucerito que a mí me	The morning star that gave me
alumbraba	light
ya no está conmigo.	Is no longer here.
No quiero que me des ná,	Don't give me a thing:
sino que vengas a verme	Just come to see me
siempre que tengas lugá.	Whenever you have time.

GLOSSARY

afición: Pure, disinterested enthusiasm.

aficionado: One who enacts this enthusiasm either as a practitioner (*práctico*) or as a witness (*teórico*).

cabal: The supreme type of *aficionado*, the highest rank in the flamenco hierarchy. Although the *cabal* is a traditionalist, he is not a rigid dogmatist closed to valid innovations. Mere knowledge does not make a *cabal*. He must have a unique sensibility, a rich psyche, and an unusual integrity.

cambio: A transition within the same generic style to a more dramatic, difficult version.

cantaor general: A singer who performs many styles well as opposed to the one who has poured all of his flamenco potential into two or three styles.

cante: Generic name for flamenco singing or song, used rather than *canto* or *canción*. The addition of the word *flamenco* is not needed.

cante de preparación: In the "suite" of songs common to several styles the first preparatory song, lowest in dramatic pitch, shortest in length, least difficult to perform. A prologue for the ascending drama to come.

compadre: Intimate friend, godfather.

copita: Diminutive of *copa*, small glass for wine or liquor.

duende: In the words of Federico García Lorca, "that which has black sounds has *duende*. . . . It is a power, a struggle for creation in act. . . . The *duende* must be awakened in the ultimate rooms of the blood." The struggle for and with *duende* is what creates the emotion in *cante flamenco*. Therefore, the singer must "risk" everything. It is the marrow of form rather than the visible outer part of form.

enamorado: A lover of something; a lover of *cante*, of the bullfight, etc.

entendido: Very knowledgeable *aficionado*.

exponerse: To expose one's innermost feelings and physical capacities during the performance of a song, absolutely necessary in the search for *duende*.

facultades: Physical resources such as strong lungs, wide tonal range, melodic facility. More essential than these for the flamenco singer is the capacity to transmit his deeper feelings. Often, *facultades* and too much technique hinder this transmission.

fin de fiesta: Spectacular series of songs or combination of song and dance ending a session or a flamenco "show."

flamencona: Super *flamenca*, a woman always ready to party.

fonda: Inn, eating house.

jaleo: Traditional form of response and accompaniment of the witness. This includes hand clapping, finger popping, heel-and-toe tapping, knuckle rapping, and the following set vocal phrases which correspond to the achievement and struggle of the singer:

> *ole:* Believed by some to be derived from Arabic *Allah*, in flamenco it crowns a superior effort.

178

eso es: Literally, "That's it," meaning the singer is on the right path.

valiente: Literally, "Courageous one," crowning a difficult physical passage.

vamos allá: Literally, "Let's go there," designed to spur the singer on to greater effort.

sí señor: Literally, "Yes sir," praise one notch above *eso es*.

jipío: Weeping, sobbing, hiccuping sound, defiant or pathetic, often in the middle of the sung line.

juerga: Often used as a generic name for flamenco session, but should be distinguished from the more serious "closed-door session"; *juerga* has a tendency to become wild, uncontrolled fiesta; often occurs in the later stage of a "closed-door session."

macho: The completion of a series of songs of the same generic style by a supremely difficult rendition within the same style or, in some cases, another one.

melisma: Extending and prolonging notes over a given syllable; not to be confused with *jipío*, the *melisma* is more flowing, as for example in the *malagueña*.

nada: Nothing, as in *No dice nada*, "He's saying nothing."

niño bonito: Spoiled "pretty boy."

paseo: Classical evening promenade of sweethearts or potential sweethearts in gardens, squares, or main streets of Andalusian towns.

pelear con el cante: To fight or struggle with the song.

pellizco: Literally, "pinch," but in flamenco argot, the hair-raising feeling that a singer causes by a certain stress or ascending dramatic move. The *pellizco* is a landmark of *duende* country.

pícaro: Rogue, rascal, hustler.

por: For, by, through; also meaning "in the manner of." For example, the singer may ask the guitarist to play *por soleares* and then spontaneously choose one of the many styles within that genre.

posada: Inn, tavern.

rajo: Raucous, harsh quality and timbre of the voice, suitable for many flamenco styles.

remate: The way of ending a line, a song, or a "suite" of songs which completes and heightens the drama.

romper la voz: Literally, to break the voice; to cast aside the smooth exterior sound and to enter the deeper provinces.

salida: Melismatic nonverbal prologue to the opening line; follows the *temple*. The *salida* alone will reveal to the knowing witness the superiority or deficiency of a singer and announce his particular temperamental vision of a given style.

sesión a puertas cerradas: The closed door session, ideal ambiance in which to preserve ritualistic intimacy and allow the authentic flamenco elements to unfold.

simpático: Charming, friendly, open.

tapas: Hors d'oeuvres served with wine or beer.

temple: The tuning of the voice and the psychic preparation that precedes the opening *ay*, the *salida*, or the first line.

testigo: The participating witness. In flamenco there is no spectator or passive listener but rather an active witness.

tirar pa' dentro: Literally, "to pull towards the inside": the sound must be pulled inside and then released.

vino fino: One of the lighter dry sherry wines ideal for the mellow flamenco mood.

BIBLIOGRAPHY

Following is a selection from the works I have read. For a more complete guide to the flamenco literature see the bibliography by González Climent.

Borrow, George. *The Zincali, or An Account of the Gypsies in Spain*. London: John Murray, 1893. (Originally published in England in 1841.)

Brown, Irving Henry. *Deep Song: Adventures with Gypsy Songs and Singers in Andalusia and Other Lands, with Original Translations*. New York: Harper & Bros., 1929.

Caba, Carlos, and Pedro Caba. *Andalucía: Su comunismo y su cante jondo*. Madrid: Biblioteca Atlántico, 1933.

Estébanez Calderón, Serafín. *Escenas andaluzas*. Barcelona: Montaner y Simón, 1945.

García Lorca, Federico. *Obras Completas*. Madrid: Aguilar, 1960. See especially "Poema del cante jondo," pp. 223–70; "El cante jondo," pp. 1514–31; and "Arquitectura del cante jondo," pp. 1537–42.

———. *Poet in New York*. New York: Grove Press, 1955. The essay there on pp. 154–66 appears also in the Aguilar *Obras Completas*, pp. 36–48, as "Teoría y juego del duende."

González Climent, Anselmo. *Andalucía en los toros, el cante y la danza*. Madrid: Imprenta Sánchez Leal, 1953.

———. *Bibliografía flamenca*. Madrid: Escelicer, 1965.

———. *Bulerías: Un ensayo jerezano*. Jerez de la Frontera: Cátedra de Flamencología, 1961.

———. *Cante en Córdoba*. Madrid: Escelicer, 1957.

———. *Flamencología*. Madrid: Imprenta Sánchez Leal, 1955. (Second edition, Madrid: Escelicer, 1964.)

———. *¡Oído al cante!* Madrid: Escelicer, 1960.

———. *Segunda bibliografía flamenca*. In collaboration with José Blas Vega. Málaga: Publicaciones de La Librería Anticuaria "El Guadalhorce," 1966.

Kahn, Máximo José. "Cante jondo y cantares sinagogales," *Revista del Occidente*, No. 88 (October 1930). Also in English, Rose Freeman, trans. *Andalusian Popular Chant and Synagogue Music*. New York: Oriole Press, 1956.

Lafuente, Rafael. *Los gitanos, el flamenco y los flamencos*. Barcelona: Editorial Barna, 1955.

Luna, José Carlos de. *De cante grande y cante chico*. Madrid: Escelicer, 1942.

———. *Gitanos de la Bética*. Madrid: Ediciones y Publicaciones Españoles, S.A., 1951.

Luque Navajas, José. *Málaga en el cante*. Málaga: Librería Anticuaria el Guadalhorce, 1965.

Machado y Álvarez, Antonio. *Cantes flamencos*. Buenos Aires: Espasa-Calpe, 1947.

———. *Colección de cantes flamencos recogidos y anotados por Demófilo*. Seville: Imprenta el Porvenir, 1881.

Manfredi Cano, Domingo. *Geografía del cante jondo*. Madrid: Colección El Grifón, 1955.

Molina, Ricardo. *Mundo y formas del cante flamenco*. Revista del Occidente, 1963.

Plata, Juan de la. *Flamencos de Jerez*. Jerez de la Frontera: Cátedra de Flamencología, 1961.

Pohren, D. E. *The Art of Flamenco*. La Mesa, Calif.: H. Howell. (Published in Jerez de la Frontera: Cátedra de Flamencología, 1962.)

————. *Lives and Legends of Flamenco: A Biographical History*. La Mesa, Calif.: H. Howell. (Published in Seville: Society of Spanish Studies.)

Triana, Fernando el de. *Arte y artistas flamencos*. Madrid: Imprenta Helénica, 1935. (Second edition, Madrid: Editorial Clan, 1952.)

DISCOGRAPHY

The following list is a selection of a few choice long-playing records mainly featuring the singers mentioned in this book.

Anthology of Cante Flamenco. London, 1960 (A-4353, 33 1/3 rpm, 3 records). Featuring Antonio Mairena and Aurelio Sellés.

Antología de los cantes de Cádiz. Madrid: Hispavox, 1960 (HH-10-193, 33 1/3 rpm). Featuring Aurelio Sellés.

Antología del cante flamenco. Madrid: Hispavox, 1956 (HH-12-03, 33 1/3 rpm, 3 records). Two songs by Pepe "El de la Matrona."

Antonio Mairena, La gran historia del cante gitano andaluz. San Sebastian: Columbia Records, 1966 (MCE-814-816, 33 1/3 rpm, 3 records).

Antonio Mairena, La llave de oro del cante flamenco. Madrid: Hispavox, 1964 (HH-10-251, 33 1/3 rpm).

Aurelio Sellés. Madrid: Hispavox, 1962 (HH-10-194, 33 1/3 rpm).

Café Chinitas. Madrid: Hispavox, 1964 (HH-10-259, 33 1/3 rpm). Songs by Diego Beijveder Morilla and Ángel Luiggi.

Cantes de Antonio Mairena. Madrid: Columbia Records, 1958 (CCCD-31010, 33 1/3 rpm).

Cantes de Málaga. Madrid: Cor, 1962 (F-210, 33 1/3 rpm). Includes Manolillo "El Herraor" singing "El Piyayo."

Diego el Perote. Madrid: Hispavox, 1965 (HH-16-502, 45 rpm). Malagueñas.

Diego el Perote, El cante por malagueñas. Madrid: Columbia Records, 1967 (SCGE-8123, 45 rpm).

El cante de don Antonio Chacón. Barcelona: Odeón (DSOE-16-488, 45 rpm).

El cante de Manolo Caracol. Madrid: RCA, 1958 (LDLP-1054, 33 1/3 rpm).

José Meneses. RCA Victor Española, 1965 (LPM-10300, 33 1/3 rpm).

Juan de la Loma. Madrid: Hispavox, 1965 (HH-16-502, 45 rpm).

La Niña de los Peines. Barcelona: RCA (7-EPL-13-314, 7-EPL-13-230, 45 rpm, 2 records).

Los ases del flamenco. Barcelona: RCA (7-EPL-13-235, 7-EPL-13-365, 2 records). Featuring Tomás Pavón, Manolo Caracol, and Vallejo.

Pepe el de la Matrona. Madrid: Hispavox, 1960 (HC-46-04, 45 rpm).

Selección antológica del cante flamenco. Madrid: Telefunken, 1958 (TFJ-95511-13, 45 rpm, 3 records). Directed by Perico "El Lunar."

Sevilla: Cuna del cante flamenco. Madrid: Columbia Records, 1959 (CCLP-31008, 33 1/3 rpm). Featuring La Fernanda de Utrera, La Bernarda de Utrera, Juan Talegas, Antonio Mairena.

Terremoto. Barcelona: Phillips, 1962 (421-213-PE, 45 rpm).

Una historia del cante flamenco. Madrid: Hispavox, 1958 (HH-1023-4, 33 1/3 rpm, 2 records). Featuring Manolo Caracol; excellent essay by M. Marcia Matos; available in United States under the Washington label.

About the Author

Born in 1927, Paul Hecht grew up and was educated in New York City. He attended Brooklyn College, where Miguel Pizarro and M. J. Benardete kindled his interest in Spanish language and literature. After obtaining his M.A. in romance languages in 1951, he went to Mexico for two years of further study.

In 1957, Mr. Hecht made his first trip to Spain and has lived in Málaga intermittently ever since. He has written articles on flamenco for Spanish newspapers and has also lectured at the University of Madrid and Brooklyn College.